Niranjan,

From all of the team at
Zurich, something to remind
you of your time in sunny
Swindon.

All the very best for the
future.

Nick

Scott

SWINDON
An Illustrated History

MARK CHILD

breedon **books** PUBLISHING

First published in Great Britain in 2002 by
The Breedon Books Publishing Company Limited
Breedon House, 3 The Parker Centre,
Derby, DE21 4SZ.

ISBN 1 85983 322 5

Printed and bound by Butler & Tanner, Frome,
Somerset, England.

Cover printing by Lawrence-Allen Colour Printers,
Weston-super-Mare, Somerset, England.

CONTENTS

Dedication

This book is dedicated to my children, and to my
wife Lorraine.

Also to the memory of George Strange (1843–1925),
the irascible, curmudgeonly, but totally intriguing
higgler of Hook; one-time pugilist and father of 27
children, who was her great-grandfather.

At most hostelries mentioned in this book his whistle
was not only wetted, but thoroughly soaked.

FOREWORD

Swindon has been well represented in pictures. In 1979 Peter Sheldon published a book of historic photographs with captions. Over the next decade, this developed into a series, mostly under his own imprint, Red Brick Publishing. In 1988 The Swindon Society began a similar series, which has continued into the new millennium. It is now possible for readers to see Swindon as it was, through hundreds of images. This book is an attempt to provide an illustrated, written history, roughly in chronological order, for those who like also to read about the town's past. I hope this present volume is a reasonable overview; a flavour of the town's long history, occasionally stopping off at some point in time or place that may be of particular interest. Yet I can hardly hope to even scratch the surface of the topics I have chosen to write about. The story of Swindon's fairs and markets, for example, would alone fill a book this size. In the Afterword, there are suggestions for how you might pursue an interest in aspects of Swindon's history. All the historic photographs are used, with permission, from the collection in Swindon's reference library. They have no known copyright and, in most cases, the photographer is also unknown.

INTRODUCTION

The common misconception is that Swindon did not exist at all before the mid-19th century. There are several reasons for this, the main one being the generalisation that 'Swindon was always a railway town'. In fact, it was a thriving community for centuries before the railways came, and it ceased to be dependent on them decades ago. Certainly, the needs of the Great Western Railway works enabled an independent, new town from the 1840s. This settlement grew alongside those works and was for decades largely populated by its employees, and others who marketed essential products and services to them. Today it is a centre for cutting edge information technology, and attracts a huge range of high-tech industries. It is simply that old adages die hard, even if the proof of their error is plain. Swindon has been so inextricably linked to what it became in the industrial sense, that many people are surprised to learn that it is a very old settlement indeed. The hill on which old Swindon stands was known to prehistoric man who farmed close to it,

Looking towards New Swindon, *c.*1885. This is a view, taken across the fields, of the plain south of the railway village and the works. The two landmarks are St Mark's Church and the GWR water tower in Bristol Street. Neat hay ricks in the middle distance underline the rural nature of the scene which, by the end of the 19th century, would be transformed by streets as the new town expanded to the south-west.

Wick Farmhouse. This is typical of the lowland farmsteads that grew up around Swindon hill. However, Wick Farm lies just off Hay Lane, a prehistoric trackway. There is evidence that the site may have been occupied from Roman times; and a reference to 'la Wik' here in the 13th century. It was almost certainly occupied by the 14th century, and there was a farm here in the 16th. The house itself dates from c.1700, although it is possible that there may be remains of a mediaeval building beneath the front portion of the present structure. Indeed, this could be a very old foundation indeed, which would make it untypical of the other farms in the area. The Anglo-Saxon word 'wyk' had an especial meaning as an outlying farmstead, in particular a dairy farm. Wickes or wiches were words used in the 18th century to describe small dairy houses that provided the local community with butter or cheese. At one time there were cheese lofts above the dairy to the right of the farmhouse. These, and the stables and associated outbuildings, were converted into dwellings in 1995 by a private developer who also renovated the farmhouse.

and the area has certainly been populated since Roman times. To some degree, the town's proximity to several very spectacular reminders of Wiltshire's prehistoric past – such as Avebury, the Ridgeway, Liddington Hill and Barbury Castle – has concentrated most people's minds away from its own ancient history.

There are other factors that have helped to perpetuate the myth. When the Great Western Railway Company established its locomotive, carriage and wagon works here, it also built both the property and a respectable social infrastructure that effectively allowed the new town to grow in

isolation. What's more, this was so distanced from old Swindon, and separated by distinct geographical and topographical features, that at first the new enterprise had plenty of space in which to do so. One settlement was on the top of a hill, the other in the extensive marshlands and fields to the north. Indeed, the new railway town was four times the size of its neighbour before the two were physically linked. Administratively, they were not joined until 1900. Another reason why Swindon gives the impression of being so young is the smallness and relative unimportance of the hilltop town before the 19th century. Old

Swindon was at the summit of a similar rise to those of nearby Highworth and Wootton Bassett, yet for centuries both of these settlements were larger, more populous and of greater economic viability. Swindon was frequently referred to in all manner of documents as being 'near' one or other of them, thus underlining its secondary status in the area.

Also, there is a lamentable lack of tangible evidence of the centuries. Much of what we know about hilltop Swindon, once called High Swindon because of its elevated position, comes from documents. Mostly these are manorial documents, which most people never see. Solid masonry, which would show that Swindon had a pre-19th century past, is slight indeed. There are the scant ruins of a mediaeval church, tucked away in parkland and mostly secured within its churchyard from public ingress. In Cricklade Street there is one of the finest remaining 18th-century façades in the county. Whatever exists of an older Swindon can mostly be found today in cellars and footings, and occasionally the re-built fabric of offices, which are not on public view. That, or it often lies buried beneath the 20th century redevelopment around the older parts of the town. Those who knew the hilltop area until a decade or so after World War Two, would have seen a number of 18th-century buildings that are no longer standing, and some that were thought to have been much older. A lot of this was sacrificed to road-widening schemes and car parks in an orgy of destruction and redevelopment during the 1960s. This has all served to support the idea that Swindon is a much younger town than it really is.

Yet we now know that people have lived, worked, played and died on the hill in more or less continuous succession for the last two millennia, and intermittently around it for much longer. That kind of occupation suggests that here was a site of greater importance than those would have us believe, who erroneously band together the two Swindons and give them a dismissive, truncated history.

As we go into the third millennium AD, earth-moving requirements for new residential and commercial estates are helping to provide a more enlightening and detailed history of Swindon's past. The discoveries of the Victorian archaeologists pale beside those of the contemporary JCB.

Ancient history

Swindon grew out of settlements around the hill about 450ft above sea level. That this appears never to have been used in a similar way to nearby fortified high ground is surprising, given its commanding position, its natural defence against attack from the north and the amount of prehistoric activity in the area. Although we know that there has been human activity hereabouts for several millennia, there is no evidence of actual habitation on the hill before the Bronze Age. Prehistoric artefacts discovered in the area are very few indeed, and can mostly be accounted for by itinerant activities. The most important of the earliest discoveries around Swindon Hill are Bronze Age burials, implements and pottery, and Iron Age artefacts. These were found in and around the sites of the old Portland and Purbeck limestone quarries.

There is archaeological evidence of isolated farmsteads in the landscape around the hill before Roman times. Most importantly, an Iron Age farm complex was discovered on the lowlands to the north in the mid-1970s. However, it was the Romans who established the first small town in the area, close to the junction of their two major roads near present-day Stratton St Margaret. This was predominantly a military town and trading post that undoubtedly supported and gave peace of mind to the Roman owners of estates and villas in the area. Evidence of their occupation has so frequently come to light that we now regard the surrounding area to the south and east of the hill as a very important part of Roman Britain. Since the mid-20th century, work on peripheral housing developments to accommodate Swindon's residential expansion has frequently disclosed archaeological evidence of Roman occupation. An extensive second century community site, discovered to the south at Groundwell Ridge, has

been called 'a real jewel in the crown of southern England'. The foundations of Roman buildings have been excavated to the north and east of the hill, in most cases also revealing pottery and coins.

The Saxons who eventually filled the property vacuum left by the recall to Rome, may well have taken over a Romano-British hilltop site later in the fifth century. Evidence of their occupation was found in the present Market Square and a little to the east of it. Here there is now a small residential development, where the remains of Anglo-Saxon, wood-framed and plaster huts were found. There is evidence that the occupants of these farmed the land and made cloth. Pottery was recovered which suggests that the site was occupied during the sixth and seventh centuries. The name given to modern-day Saxon Court not only recalls its former occupants, but is a reminder that the mediaeval settlement of Swindon most probably developed from this point. Anglo-Saxons also created land charters for apportioning their holdings around the hill. The names of places and physical features in the modern landscape can frequently be traced to the descriptions used then. For the first time, pre-Conquest, the hill is described due to the pigs that were kept on it.

Swindon at Domesday

At the Domesday survey of 1086 Suindone/dune was assessed at 21¾ hides and divided between five holdings of land. The largest was of 12 hides, held by Odin the Chamberlain, and was to become part of the mediaeval manor of High Swindon. Two smaller portions were held by Uluric and Ulward, the two-hide estate of the former most probably comprising the mediaeval manor of West Swindon. In the 1500s, High Swindon and West Swindon were joined, and became Over and Nether Swindon or West and East Swindon. In 1086, five hides belonged to

Odo, Bishop of Bayeux, Earl of Kent and half-brother of King William. These have been identified with the mediaeval manor of Nethercott, which in the 15th century was split to include Eastcott and Westcott. The former was acquired by the Vilett family in the 1700s and the latter by the Goddard family later in the 18th century. To the north-west at Domesday, Alvred (Alfred) of Marlborough had 1½ hides. There were also small estates at Walcot. The other mediaeval manors were those of Even Swindon and Broome, although it is not known when they were established. High Swindon was held by the de Valence family in the 13th century, and it was an indictment of William de Valence in 1274 that gives us the earliest clue to Swindon's status as a mediaeval market.

The earliest record of parliamentary representation is John Ildhelfe and Richard Pernaunt in 1295, and thereafter sporadically: Richard Neel in 1304, Thomas Crekkelade and Robert Crekkelade in 1422, and in 1660 Nevil Maskelyne. The figure of 248 poll tax payers recorded for 1334 suggests a healthy little market town. However, it did not develop as one might expect. The manors were all passed around over the next few hundred years by favour, disfavour and marriage until 1563, when the Manor of Swindon was acquired by Thomas Goddard whose family had been living hereabouts for some time.

Mediaeval agriculture, industry and trade were little more than one might expect of a rural settlement. The softer chalk downland to the south was ideal for grazing sheep, whereas the nutritious, if heavy, clay deposits to the north facilitated cattle and pig farming. Hides came into Swindon to be processed by the tanners and woolmongers who are occasionally mentioned in old documents. As the 17th century progresses, we read of Mathew Barber the clothworker, clothier William Heath, shearman Henry Farmer,

Laurance Stichall the mercer, cordwainers Samuel Osborne, Samuel Day and Thomas Hollegg, Richard Heath the silkweaver, and tailor Joseph Wild. Yet there was no big cloth industry in Swindon; probably just enough was done for the town's requirements. It is also remarkable that Swindon did not develop as a leather tanning centre. Tanners and curriers (such as Phillip Naish at the end of the 17th century) are mentioned only sporadically, before the mid-19th-century firm of Langfield & Greenaway briefly supplied the town's boot and shoe trade, and saddle and harness makers. The hill itself was dominated by hard rock that was worked as building stone. Around this was sandy soil, which is why the area that led westwards from the old town past Okus became known as The Sands. Well drained, this provided good pasture and land for arable farming both on top of the hill and around its slopes.

Swindon's early street plans

It is impossible to be precise about the age of hilltop Swindon's earliest named thoroughfares. Very old trackways led on to the hill from Wroughton and Marlborough in the south. Ancient too, was the northern route between the hilltop and the lowlands, which later became the coaching road to Cricklade. It is not unreasonable to suppose that these three points would have been the first to be connected. Common to all was the Market Place which was probably planned in the 13th century, next to the old settlement, as the basis for the mediaeval market town it became over the next 100 years or so.

Newport Street joined the Wroughton trackway with the one from Marlborough, and met High Street at its eastern end, joining the Marlborough thoroughfare with the exit towards Cricklade. It has been suggested that Newport Street is the oldest thoroughfare in the town. More correctly, it

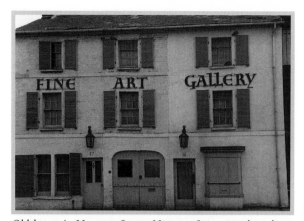

Old house in Newport Street. Newport Street may have been the site of the very first markets to be held in Swindon in the 13th century. Nothing now exists of that time. The small limewashed, thatched cottages of rough timber and undressed stone that gave the western part of the street its particularly rural appearance until well into the 20th century, were undoubtedly put up centuries later. One building remains, however, with cellars of the 14th century that are thought to be connected to the extensive honeycomb of tunnels that ran beneath the old town. Certainly one bricked up tunnel there appears to point towards the White Hart (which was certainly in existence as the Bull alehouse by 1771) almost opposite. This three-storey, three bay house (in reality two houses) is reputed to be the oldest in the town. It was for many years a gallery where fine art was displayed and painters received instruction at the hands of the proprietor.

is the earliest that appears on extant documents, being recorded as Nyweport Street in one of 1346. The name means 'new market', giving credence to the suggestion that a market had been established on the market place and was already occupying at least one of the radiating roads. In the 14th century, the hilltop settlement was known as Hegherswyndon (High Swindon). For all that, it appears not to have progressed beyond a lane with very few intermittent dwellings for nearly five centuries. Low, thatched cottages were put up as people acquired portions of land, and the whole road gradually built up in a very piecemeal fashion. At the beginning of the 1900s the original lines of Newport Street were still intact. Many of the original cottages were still standing in the first half of the 20th century. Others, particularly towards the eastern end, were remodelled or rebuilt with brick façades and

remain today on their ancient foundations.

Newport Street retains the oldest house in Swindon. This stands above cellars that are thought to be 14th century. Other houses in the street have cellars that are also several centuries old. To the east of Newport Street is High Street, and although there are no records of this name until the end of the 16th century, the two are likely to be coeval. Further credence is given to this by the position of the Market Square, being roughly where the two roads meet. The manor estate was immediately to the east of this thoroughfare, and there was almost certainly a mediaeval house here, where later stood the Lawn, home to generations of the Goddard family, Lords of the Manor. Next to it was the 13th-century church. The latter was reached by a lane off High Street, the former by a driveway. Running west from the north end of High Street is Wood Street, also named as such from late in the 16th century. The basic road layout, then, was three sides of a virtual square. There were, of course, a few trackways; in particular Mill Lane which was certainly so called by the early 1700s and linked High Street with the millpond and mill close to Holy Rood Church.

These roads were added to, and the roads of Swindon assumed the shape of an elongated triangle. High Street extended northwards into Cricklade Street by the mid-17th century, to the point where the old coaching road dropped suddenly down the hill. This had long been known as Brock Hill, and it has been supposed that the name derived from badger setts to be found in the area. However, a map of 1763 clearly refers to this road as Brookhill, and a group of dwellings at right angles to it as Brookhill Cottages. At about the same time, a track that linked High Street with the damson orchards on the Goddard estate became Dammas Lane. At the beginning of the 19th century, a Mr

Canford House, Devizes Road. Built *c.*1840 with its attractive wrought iron porch, this was Swindon's police house for many years. Joseph Hall was the first police superintendent to live here, as did his successor Henry Haynes who held such offices as Inspector of the Nuisance Removal Committee, and Assistant Relieving Officer for Vagrants. He was also an officer of both the Old Swindon and New Swindon Local Boards. According to Frederick Large in his 1931 book of personal reminiscences, *A Swindon Retrospect*, there was a superintendent, an inspector and two constables in the old town during the first half of the 1860s, and one sergeant in New Swindon. This is corroborated by letters to the *Swindon Advertiser* which complained about the length of time it took for reinforcements to arrive from the hill top when there were problems in New Swindon. The police station in Eastcott Hill was opened in 1873 and the superintendent there, George North, was a friend of writer Richard Jefferies. North had to read the Civil Riot Act from the Town Hall, Old Swindon at the time of the General Election in April 1880, when Swindon was still in the Cricklade constituency. Police squad cars in Swindon were first fitted with radios in 1949, and the town's policemen on the beat first used two-way radios on 17 February 1966; the first force in Wiltshire to have them.

Tidd lived here, who was paid 6d a year for shutting the nearby church door. Exactly how and when Devizes Road came about (joining the west ends of Newport Street and Wood Street) is unknown, mainly because it remained a lane with no dwellings along it until well into the 19th century. A roadway that was to become known as Little London and its extension, Back Lane, joined the west end of Wood Street with Cricklade Street. To the west of Wood Street, a lane descended King's Hill on its way to Wootton Bassett, and another ran north from it towards the hamlet of Eastcott. This, then, was Swindon's basic street plan until the 19th century.

Swindon around 1700

It is possible to understand life in Swindon before the end of the 18th century only with a lot of conjecture and by applying information known about similar country towns at the time. There was no complete census at the beginning of the 1700s, but an academic guess, based on an ecclesiastical count made a quarter of a century earlier, might be a little over 600 men, women and children. Twenty-six freeholders were listed in 1705; a rental of monies due to the Lord of the Manor, only on Michaelmas Day, in 1717 lists 45 names, and there were an additional 34 leaseholders whose rents were due on both Lady Day and Michaelmas Day. By 1772 the number of freeholders had risen to 41, and several of the family lines were well established. Extant lists of Swindon's inhabitants, made around the start of the 1700s, do provide brief snapshots. What they suggest, is a very small, remarkably self-contained settlement whose inhabitants created their own internal economy with very little outside influence. The source of revenue was local agriculture, livestock and stone quarrying. With the exception of the church, the parish clerks, and a couple of bailiffs, there were no service industries. Those who were neither gentry on private incomes at one end of the social chain, nor receiving alms at the other, were either employed in recognised manual trades or were labourers. Some of the latter appear to have been living in very difficult conditions, even in premises owned by the Manor. Several of the entries in the rentals of monies due to the Goddards from leaseholders of their properties record that the house had 'fallen in'. We also read in the early 1700s of Richard York, paying eight pence a year for 'his house late a barn'.

Trades in Swindon were only those needed either to process the products of the labouring

Warehouse, Market Square. High up on one side of this building are the words 'A.W. Deacon's Corn Stores'. It is likely that north Wiltshire cheese was once made in cheese lofts on the second level. There were a couple of cottages here before this four-storey building was put up early in the 19th century. Quite early in its existence the building was owned by Phillip Pavey, the miller of Elcombe, Wroughton, who converted it into a corn, manure and general agricultural dealership. Mr Deacon took over the business, and remained there until 1850 when it was acquired by John Toomer, a coal and salt merchant who set up his own business at the New Swindon railway station in 1849. Toomer soon added coke, lime and hay to his merchandise, and a depot in Bath Road. A corn, seed and forage merchant occupied this building into the 1990s when it was the last direct, tangible link with the old town's 19th-century Corn Market.

class or provide for the town at a very basic level. The retail mix was severely limited, little more than was needed to clothe and feed the inhabitants. Indeed, the town did not have a grocer, independent of the provisions sold at the weekly market, until Robert and Margaret Boxwell set up one in High Street in about 1705.

(This was eventually incorporated into the Bull Inn, and then became part of Mason's grocery emporium.) Half a century later, this business was still obtaining its produce locally with the exceptions only of tea and sugar which came from London. The insularity of Swindon is also recognisable in family names. Very many spellings at the beginning of the 18th century, and indeed for the best part of the next two, can be traced back for hundreds of years in Swindon's manorial documents. Swindon was not a town that its occupants readily moved from or changed.

The biggest single source of employment as the 17th century ended was undoubtedly the local quarries, for in 1701, 15 Swindon roughmasons or stonecutters were listed. There was a considerable pool of around 40 labourers that nonetheless changed, to a degree, year-on-year. Some of these probably worked at the quarries. One comes across the occasional labourer who later turns up in a recognised trade, having bettered himself or shown an entrepreneurial streak. Bartholemew King, for example, clearly thought that the town could sustain more than the two butchers reported in 1697. Within a couple of years he had taken on the role. William Naish, then a labourer, soon became a recognised mason. Nicholas Noad, listed as a labourer, was elsewhere referring to himself as gardener, soon to become a specified trade in the town.

It might be reasonable to say that the average Swindonian's diet in 1700 consisted of bread, meat and beer. There were four bakers in the town (who would surely have been supplied by miller Oliver Farmer), four butchers, five named innholders and various ale sellers. However, the actual number of beer sellers and the true status of their houses is unknown.

The Sharpes family of coopers, and barrel-maker Joseph Coventry supplied the containers required by the public houses and victuallers.

Just south of the Wilts & Berks Canal, roughly where Corporation Street is now, stood the hamlet of Eastcott. It is mentioned in deeds going back to the 13th century, and regularly from the 17th. The tortuous trackway that connected it with the Sands on the hilltop, began there as Eastcott Lane; a thoroughfare which before the 1850s had only the occasional cottage and a couple of farmsteads along its length. In theory, this was a road that might have been developed between Old Swindon and New Swindon in preference to Victoria Street, for whereas the latter petered out into orchards, the Eastcott track had long been a well trod route. Its main buildings in the 19th century were the Prospect Works, where William Affleck made agricultural implements and machinery, and the impressive and vaguely Italianate police station of 1873 that remained operative for 100 years. Not until the last two decades of that century was Eastcott Lane to be built up on its western side, although its continuation, Eastcott Hill, was terraced on both sides from the 1850s, almost to its intersection with present day Crombey Street. Thereafter, the route remained substantially unpopulated, connecting Upper Eastcott Farm, Lower Eastcott Farm and the hamlet of Eastcott. This photograph is of Eastcott Hill Cottages in 1964. It illustrates how this road looked as it began to be built up during the second half of the 19th century. Despite the fact that it was a major thoroughfare between New Swindon and the old town, it was not lit until the mid-1860s, when gas lamps were put in place.

Other than that, the variety of retailers was small and there were generally only one or two examples of each. William Restall was the town's only mercer. Will and Ben Lawrence were respectively the draper and glover, the latter no doubt associated with currier Phillip Naish – as would also have been sadler Joseph Deacon. Hereabouts has always been great sheep country, and Roger Brown, Edward Hinton and John Howse made a living out of weaving in Swindon. More than one writer was later to remark on the unusually high number of Swindon residents who lived in easy circumstances. Perhaps the number of servants recorded, about 20 for each of the years around the beginning of the 18th century, attests to the amount of affluence in the town even then.

The patronage of those people who were better off helped to support four tailors; but the effects of uneven roads on everyone, and the hard lifestyle of the labouring classes, meant good work for the town's ten boot and shoe makers.

Other trades associated with the rural nature of the town around 1700 included four blacksmiths, two carpenters, a chandler, a cheese factor, a joiner, two slaters and a wheelwright. There was also an ironmonger and a glazier. The fabric of the church was apparently in decline, for the churchwarden's accounts refer to repairs to the church walls and costs associated with glazing and replastering. Some 20 persons – mostly widows – were receiving alms, and the medical care of the town fell to surgeon Joseph Heath.

Tolls and turnpikes

The four main access roads into Swindon were all turnpiked between 1751 and 1775 and so continued until highway districts were formed, following the Highway Act, 1862. For example, in 1757, the Act was applied to the road between Swindon and Faringdon; that between Swindon and Marlborough was turnpiked in 1761. There were to be toll houses on the roads to Stratton, Marlborough, Devizes, Wootton Bassett and Cricklade, and another in Regent Street. Those on the Stratton Road and the Marlborough Road were two-storey buildings. For private travellers, the amount levied depended on the type of conveyance (carriage, cart, coach or wagon), the number of horses used, and the width of the wheels involved. Basically, the narrower the wheel, the more expensive it was to travel. This related to the state of the roads, in that narrower wheels dug deeper, thereby necessitating more costly repairs to the surface. For the same reason, the cost of drawing heavy millstones along the highway was prohibitive. Later, charges were

standardised for wagons, carts, chaises, gigs, carriages, horses, mules or asses, calves, sheep, pigs and general 'beasts'. The difficulty here was that each road was turnpiked by a different trust, the Commissioners licensing the trusts by auction held either at The Crown/Goddard Arms or latterly at the Town Hall in the Market Square. The actual running of the gates was usually sub-contracted to women by the successful bidders. A ticket bought at a particular toll house was valid at others run by the same trust, provided the journey was made within the same 24 hours. Prices paid bore little relation to distance travelled. For example, a ticket bought at the Groundwell toll gate gave free passage only at Eastcott Lane. However, if you were off to Cricklade, a ticket bought at the King's Hill toll gate took you freely through those at Purton, Widham, Packhorse, Chelworth, Lane Bar, Newth's, Liddiard Marsh and Cricklade Dance. Apart from the routes into the town already mentioned, there was a thoroughfare that connected Stratton with the road to Cricklade, and the residents of Rodbourne Cheney and the Liddiards came via roadways that linked Shaw and Rushey Platt with King's Hill.

Roads around Swindon were kept clean by means of dividing them into lots and auctioning the 'road scrapings and parings' to individuals who might subsequently be able to sell whatever they took up. Exactly how this worked in 1846, can be gleaned from an advertisement placed by auctioneers Dore & Fidel for a sale to be held 'precisely at four o'clock in the afternoon', at the Goddard Arms. Bids were taken on the following lots, which were sold for a period of 11 calendar months.

'1, From Swindon to the top of Kingshill. 2, From thence to the canal. 3, From thence to the hand post at Mannington. 4, From thence to the brow of the hill at Whitehill. 5, From thence to the Lodge Gate. 6, From thence to the west corner of Agbourn Coppice. 7, From thence to the Fourth Mile-stone. 8, From thence to the Gate, in the occupation of Ann Rudler. 9, From thence to the stream of water crossing the road by William Watt's. 10, From thence to the Turnpike Gate. 11, From thence to the borough of Wootton Bassett. Swindon Parish Road. 12, From Mr Blackford's Corner to the Wharf Bridge, and 13, The scraping and sweeping of all the streets in the Town of Swindon.'

Number 13 clearly meant the most work, but held the potential for the richest pickings. Whoever bought it was subject to an additional condition, namely, that the sweepings had to be removed every Thursday and Saturday, 'and at any other time the Surveyor may direct'. The Surveyor and Assistant Overseer at the time was William Read. Given that all the markets and fairs in Swindon were then held on Mondays, one can only guess at the state of the roads by Thursday!

The Goddard estate

The Goddard family was certainly in Swindon at the start of the 15th century. Thomas Goddard of Upham acquired a manor here in 1562, and

The Lawn, off High Street. This building and its mediaeval predecessor were home to the Goddard family, Lords of the Manor of Swindon. Thomas Goddard acquired manorial rights in 1563 and held the title for four years. Thereafter, it passed from father to son until 1732. Known dates are: Richard Goddard (from 1568), Thomas (until 1641), Richard (1644–50), Thomas (1651–83) and Richard (until 1732). The latter Thomas was a minor until 1669. His mother Anne was appointed as his guardian until 1656, when the job passed to Thomas Bowman. In 1732, the title passed to Richard's brother Pleydell Goddard who held it for ten years; then to Pleydell's cousin Ambrose Goddard (1745–54). Ambrose's two sons then held the manor in succession; Thomas (1757–70) and his brother Ambrose (1771–1815). The latter's son, Ambrose Lethbridge Goddard, followed (1852–95), and was succeeded by his son Fitzroy Pleydell Goddard (1895–1927). He was the last of the male line to live in Swindon.

Gazebo, the Lawn. The gazebo overlooks an area that was pasture land for cattle, separated from the lawns on the Goddard estate by a ha ha; a wall and sunken ditch that kept the beasts on their field. In 1860, a particularly fine ox from this field of about 70 horned cattle, was found dead, and seven others appeared to have been poisoned, necessitating prompt action to 'save their livers'. It transpired that instead of burning or mulching the grass cuttings and shrub trimmings from the estate, the gardener had been in the habit of throwing them into the ha-ha. On this occasion, he had included some yew cuttings which had been eaten by the unfortunate beasts.

members of the family were lords of the manor from then until the 20th century. What Thomas bought was clearly set down; it included the profits of the fairs and the weekly market, 60 messuages, 40 cottages, 2 water mills, 100 gardens, 100 orchards, 600 acres of land, 200 acres of meadow, 1,000 acres of heath, 30 acres of woods, 120 acres of pasture and one dovecote.

The Goddard family estate, reached by a main driveway off High Street, was laid out about 1800 around the manor house of c.1770. It is likely that this was put up on the site of a mediaeval

building, on an eminence surrounded by fields. Part of the gateway pillars and entrance arches remain off High Street, although the rectangular, single-storey, classical lodges of four bays with flat pilasters were taken down in 1963. Called 'Swindon House', until 1850, and since known as the Lawn, the family home was a double-cube fronted building of brick with magnificent stone dressings and a baluster parapet topped by large pineapple and urn finials. To the east of this was a five-bedroom/dining block that looked out on to pretty garden beds and borders. When rebuilt in the late 1770s, the house must have presented an awesome sight to the townspeople as they trekked down the little lane towards the adjacent church.

Internally, when last occupied by the family, the Lawn had an outer hall and an inner hall on the ground floor, giving access to a lobby and drawing room, a dining room with an adjoining study, billiard room, library and gun room. There were two staircases leading to, amongst others, the Green Room, Rose Room, Blue Room, Major Goddard's room with dressing room adjoining, the nursery and the servants' quarters. It was furnished on a grand scale with paintings in most of the rooms and along the walls of the corridors, statuary and ornamental silverware everywhere and a large accumulation of books.

On one side of the house there was an arboretum with laid out walks; sweeping lawns with a vista of the distant, artificial lakes. These lawns were used by the Goddards for entertaining, garden parties and fêtes. When the lakes froze over sufficiently during severe winters, mass skating and winter games were enjoyed by the family and local residents. The view from the bay windows of the drawing room and those of the adjacent orangery was of a sunken Italian garden. This was formal in design but informally planted. It had severely clipped topiary and was enclosed by an open balustrade wall punctuated by

Lakes, the Lawn. The lakes are part of the Georgian redevelopment of the parkland, and are central to the delightful landscaped gardens. They were artificially created following the 18th-century remodelling of the manor house, and may have been constructed around a smaller, much older pond. In 2002 it is thought that they could be pivotal in attracting tourism to Swindon as part of a redevelopment package for the whole Lawn area. This could be part of a programme aimed at giving the grounds a much greater role in the economic and social regeneration of Old Town. As a green space it has no equal in the town, yet it is relatively under used. The grounds could be redeveloped in a way that retained their essential character but utilised the potential of features such as the lakes, for added attractions on a tourist scale.

Kathleen, left Swindon in 1931 and the house remained unoccupied until it was taken over by British and American forces during World War Two. They did not treat it well. In 1947, Swindon Corporation paid £16,000 for the 53-acre parklands, including the derelict manor house and the remains of Holy Rood Church. The house became ruinous and was demolished in 1952, by which time it had become dangerous. The grounds were opened as a public parkland, and remain pleasure grounds to this day. The gazebo is intact and there is also a ha-ha. All that remains of the Lawn is the site of the sunken garden with the bowl of the fountain, some stone pediments, the reinforced embankment and parts of the balustraded garden wall.

A small stone lodge at the entrance to the Goddard estate on Old Mill Lane, was demolished in the late 1960s. The present auctioneers' sale rooms on The Planks were originally the stables belonging to the Goddard estate. They were also on the main route taken by pedestrians between High Street and the old parish church. The raised stone causeway that runs the length of The Planks was built because walkers were seriously inconvenienced by muddy feet whenever the track flooded in wet weather.

No doubt the presence of the stables added to the discomfiture, for this was also the way horses were walked to and from the church pond, where they were washed. The fine, three-bay, 18th-century stone vicarage that stood nearly opposite the stables, was demolished in 1973.

decorative urns on pedestals. On the south side, this wall, covered with ivy over the years, masked a sheer drop that was invisible from the gardens. It also provided a backdrop for other ornamental gardens that were laid out beneath.

The driveway from High Street curved towards the garden, flanked by urns, then ran alongside the wall to the front of the house, where it ended in steps down to the arboretum. A gazebo was built, possibly above an ice house, on a rise to the east in the 1850s. It has a pyramidal roof, is thought to have utilised bricks from the tower of the lately demolished Holy Rood Church and was built to the same base dimensions. In spring, when surrounded by daffodils, the gazebo is a particularly pretty sight.

The last of the male line to live at the Lawn, Major Fitzroy Pleydell Goddard, a one-time diplomat, died in 1927. His widow, Eugenia

Smuggling and Moonrakers

Swindon may well have as strong a claim as any to the Wiltshire Moonraker legend. This tale – from which true-born Wiltshire men are known as 'Moonrakers' – is derived from the time when gangs of contraband liquor smugglers contrived to keep one step ahead of the excise men. Throughout the 16th and 17th centuries, Dutch and Flemish wool merchants were in Swindon, negotiating for wool which came from the sheep of the surrounding Wiltshire downs. They almost certainly ran the Bell in High Street which is said to have been established in 1515 and was known as the Lapwing until at least 1649.

Considerable import duty was charged on their favourite drink. A smuggling organisation was established, landing, in particular, barrels of gin and brandy, and supplies of tobacco on quiet stretches and coves of the Hampshire coast. This merchandise was destined for the great wool producing areas, in particular the Cotswolds, where the merchants had agents. But it also came to Swindon, where the merchants conducted business for the wool from the large flocks of sheep on the nearby Marlborough Downs. The fastest route for the smugglers was straight through Wiltshire; it was operated by local people who took their share, and who managed to hide the contraband in all manner of places when the heat was on. Church crypts, cellars and even ponds are said to have been involved. Legend says that one moonlit night a number of smugglers were raking up their kegs from a pond when they were surprised by excise men. Pretending to be simpletons, the former pointed to the reflection of the moon in the water and claimed they were trying to raise the cheese that had clearly fallen in. On hearing this, the government officials rode off, convinced that such unworldly persons could not be up to anything nefarious.

It is quite likely that Swindonians made gin and also supplied the local retail outlets. A warren of tunnels was constructed beneath Swindon; some have been destroyed, others bricked up, but a few remain to this day. They were part of a very comprehensive network which linked certain old buildings in the town and were used by the smugglers both as a significant warehouse and convenient escape routes. The extent of this activity can be gauged by the number of buildings known to have been so linked. These included the cellars of the White Horse – now No.42 Cricklade Street, the Goddard Arms (formerly the Crown), the King of Prussia (then the King's Head), the Bell and the Mason's Arms – all in High Street, the Georgian private house with 14th-century cellars in Newport Street, the cottages that were on the site of the old Town Hall and Corn Exchange in the Market Square, and even the Lawn which is thought to have been built on the site of a mediaeval manor house. The cellars of 19 Newport Street, thought to be the oldest house extant in Swindon, are mediaeval and may have been built by Dutch merchants engaged in the wool trade. Directly opposite stood the White Hart inn. The cellars of both buildings were joined by an underground tunnel, the southern end of which remains, although it is now bricked up.

Almost from the moment the Town Hall was built, its ground floor and cellars were occupied by a firm of wine merchants (Brown & Nephew; latterly Brown & Plummer). One day, a cellar floor collapsed and revealed what appeared to be undercrofts with grilles in them. Coloured water which was put down the grilles, reappeared in the lake on the Goddard estate. That suggested that this stretch of water might also have had some connection with the old Swindon tunnels, the smuggling activities and – who knows – the Moonraker legend.

Holy Rood Church, the Lawn. The grounds of the old church remain, but there is now no real churchyard to speak of. However, there was once a memorial to two lives of considerable longevity. 'In memory of John Alexander who died 18th May 1697 aged 117 years and also Ann his wife who died 21st March 1698 aged 98.' In 2002 it is sad to see the remains of Holy Rood church barred to the general public, by locks, chains and substantial wire fencing that effectively prevents free access. It is a sign of the times that in this comparatively isolated spot, the old walls that surround the grounds have been the object of vandalism, and the immediate environs the place of nefarious activities. One cannot help thinking that in the hands of a private developer of leisure activities, this site would be very different. Holy Rood could be maintained and protected as an integral part of a leisure scheme that would attract tourists to the former Goddard estate behind High Street.

Holy Rood Church

Close to the site of the Lawn are the remains of Holy Rood Church and the wall that stopped the churchyard from falling into the mill pond which was once almost beneath it. The public approach was from Lower Town, just south of High Street, along the way which we now call The Planks. This was also the route to the millpond, made almost impassably muddy in bad weather as the result of all manner of activities that took place there, and intolerably dusty during hot spells. Thus, a portion of the trackway was eventually raised for the convenience of pedestrians, initially boarded (hence its name) and later walled. Throughout the middle ages, people would have passed this way to use the church and churchyard for all manner of secular activities. The parish was run from the church, the priest may well have schooled the

children here, and they certainly played around the building. Oaths were taken, disputes settled and justice was meted out in the churchyard. Binding contracts were made on holy ground. Processions took place there on feast days and holy days. Whether or not trade was confined to the Market Square, since this was an early introduction in the development of Swindon, we do not know. But commonly, vendors and pedlars spread their wares for sale in the churchyard, and strolling players and musicians used it for entertainment. Some, if not all, of this would have taken place at Holy Rood.

We do not know when a church was first built here, although in 1154 it was gifted to the Priory of St Mary in Southwick, Hampshire, who supplied the rectors until 1355. A vicar, Richard de Haghemouz, is first mentioned in 1301 and the church remained dedicated to St Mary until the mid-16th century, during the incumbency of turncoat John Unthanke who was there 1527–60. One of Cromwell's generals attended a service here before the first Battle of Newbury. By 1676, some 572 Anglicans were recorded in Swindon and eight Non-conformists. The botanist and amateur astronomer James Grooby, described by William Morris as 'a venerable looking old gentleman with a studious and intelligent face', was vicar of Holy Rood 1823–47. He married into the Vilett family, in whose gift the position had been for some time.

Internally, Holy Rood appears to have been a 13th-century building, with 14th-century arcades; its external fabric was of the 15th century. There

The Planks. Stables, coach house and cottages. The Planks was a raised walkway on part of the lane that led from the Market Square in Old Swindon to a point on the Goddard estate, from where there was public access to Holy Rood Church. Until well into the 20th century, there were several buildings along its length, the most imposing of which was the former vicarage, on which site the incumbents of Holy Rood made their home for several centuries. The walkway began immediately after the entrance to the substantial vicarage garden, and remains today. In the 19th century, Ambrose Lethbridge Goddard was at loggerheads with William Read, the Old Swindon Local Board Surveyor, over posts the Lord of the Manor had set up across the roadway. The Goddard estate's 18th-century former stables and coach house, with external staircase leading to groom's attic quarters, remain unchanged externally. Built of limestone rubble, the range has a semi-hipped, tiled, mansard roof with little dormer windows. This is a very picturesque group, setting the scene for the late 18th-century Lawn Cottages that overlook the parkland. No.1 is a large, double gabled, three-bay house with attic dormer windows, built of rough limestone in a prominent position. No.2 and No.3 are made out of a run of much smaller estate workers' dwellings.

was a panelled wooden pulpit with narrow sounding board and plain moulded tester. During the eighth century, the nave was filled with box pews. However, judging from the churchwardens' accounts the fabric was in very poor condition.

There are numerous references in the churchwardens' accounts book 1770–1825 to bills for sundry repairs to the fabric, and the tower in particular regularly gave concern. Walter Taylor 'mended' it in 1770; a year later John Cook repaired and supported it, whilst Isacc Law weatherboarded the tower window. A little later, Walter Taylor was called on to 'mend' the church and Joseph Woodham to do the same for the tower. Meanwhile, William Bristow the blacksmith was mending the church door and Isacc Law the churchyard gates. In 1787, two loads of stones were brought from the Swindon quarries for use on the tower. The grounds fared no better; stonemason George Cox provided stones for the church way in 1770, and in 1792 two loads of stones came from the quarries for the churchyard wall. Fourteen years later, two local stonemasons, Richard Mills and Richard Hopkins, and William Horn, the blacksmith, were together involved in mending the road to the churchyard. In 1816 another stonemason, Richard Tarrant, was again repairing the church walk as well as the churchyard wall. At its demise, the chancel was covered in wall tablets and there were a number of hatchments in the nave.

Until the 1970s, what we knew of its appearance was mostly gleaned from drawings by Buckler and John Luckett Jefferies. Then a photograph came to light that was taken c.1847, most probably by Nevil Story-Maskelyne. He was a friend of William Henry Fox-Talbot the photographic pioneer from Lacock Abbey, who patented his negative-positive process just five years earlier. The picture showed that Holy Rood was a small building which had been partially restored in 1736. It had a low, two-stage tower that housed five bells of 1741 by Abraham Rudhall. It also had a clerestoried nave with north and south aisles, chancel with north aisle, and a south porch. It had a peal of five bells. There was an extension to the west of the south aisle, probably the vestry, that was added in 1820. The little clerestory windows were pointed, and those of the aisles were square-headed. A brick tower was erected during repairs and partial rebuilding in 1748, which cost £487 and was

mostly paid for by the sale of some church land. William Morris, Swindon's first real historian who founded the *Swindon Advertiser* in 1854, said that the tower was supported on four tree trunks. He paints a picture of a tiny building, packed out with box pews and galleries, rapidly falling into disrepair throughout the 1800s. It was described in 1830 as being 'in its exterior, of mean appearance; but the interior is fitted with great neatness, and every appropriate accommodation'.

Holy Rood was finally closed down when Christ Church was built at the northern end of the town, on the understanding that its chancel should remain, supported by the parish. The building was taken down in 1852, except for the chancel which is intact and includes a collection of repositioned wall memorials, and part of the nave arcade. The latter is a romantic ruin to this day, but usually has to be viewed from a distance as the churchyard is locked, thus discouraging spontaneous public access. There is a large table tomb beside the chancel, a memorial to several members of the Jefferies family (including two named Richard) who died throughout the 19th century. Although Swindon writer Richard Jefferies (1848–87) was a direct descendant, he is buried in Worthing, Sussex. Where there was once a nave floor, there is now a walkway paved with 18th- and 19th-century tombstones. There remains too, the vault that the Goddard family established early in the 1850s, effectively taking over the church as their private chapel and mausoleum.

In 1949, the well-being and upkeep of the ruins was assumed by Swindon Corporation, now the Borough of Swindon. For several decades the chancel was kept locked, and latterly was used as the estate groundsman's hut until 1970, in which year it was restored by Swindon Borough Council. It includes a memorial stone dated 1610 and an 18th-century tablet of Bath stone. At the restoration it was given an altar made of sections of an 18th-century table tomb from the graveyard, and a black marble cross. Ronald Packer of Bartlett Brothers, a Swindon firm of monumental masons, rebuilt the font and pulpit, and renovated and rearranged some of the memorials on the interior walls. Initially, a grille was placed over the rebuilt doorway into the chapel, so that when the building was not in use, visitors could observe but not enter. Holy Rood's chancel was re-opened the following year as an ecumenical Chapel of Unity. It is occasionally opened to the public.

Early markets

For centuries, the economy of Swindon depended on the land, and later on the success of the town's agriculture and livestock markets. William de Valence, Earl of Pembroke and half-brother of Henry III appears to have held a market without warrant in Swindon from 1259. It must have continued because in 1289 the town was designated 'Chepyng Swindon', and 'Market Swindon' in 1336. In 1626, Thomas Goddard was granted a weekly market and two fairs annually. It seems likely that this was celebrated with a market cross, first mentioned in 1662, after which date the Lord of the Manor was regularly petitioned at the Court Leet for its bad state of repair. It remained until the 19th century. The market declined into a 'petty inconsiderable one' by 1640, but its fortunes were revived when a cattle plague hit nearby Highworth 12 years later. Writing in 1672, John Aubrey remarked of Swindon, 'Here on Munday every weeke a gallant Markett for Cattle, which increased to its new greatnese upon the plague at Highworth.' By 1718, it was one of 32 weekly markets being held in Wiltshire.

In 1703, Thomas Goddard provided the first market house by ejecting some poor people receiving alms, from a former church house in High Street, converting it to a lock-up and charging an annual rent. The Swindon writer Richard Jefferies says that this building was supported by oak pillars, and was taken down in 1793 together with the town's stocks and whipping post which stood adjacent. These, as well as the square vendors' stalls in the market place, were under the care of bootmaker Henry Tarrant who held the position of Constable of Swindon for many years, before the police force was formed. By 1800, cattle sales had fallen off, although cattle were still lined up before dawn for inspection along High Street. Vendors' stalls were empty except for the weekly appearance of Mr Tidd of Dammas Lane who sold meat. The Market Square was mostly used for outdoor meetings. Notably, large crowds assembled to hear the very first Wesleyan Methodist sermon in Swindon, delivered by George Pocock of Bristol, who preached in the town until 1812.

When John Britton passed through Swindon in 1814, the population was around 1,600 in a parish of some 263 houses. There was a weekly corn market, and one every fortnight, known as the 'Great Market' for cattle. There were also five annual fairs. At the same time, a horse sale was being held in that part of the present day Devizes Road (called Horsefair until 1853) known as Shorthedge. However, Britton found that there was no particular trade carried on in the town, although he remarked on the number of persons of 'independent fortune' who lived there, and wrote of their 'mansions'. Other writers have also described the gentility of Swindon in the early 19th century. Possibly, visiting writers were spared first-hand knowledge of the town's more smelly trade, and were able to concentrate on its polite society. By the mid-1800s, the cattle market was poorly attended and had become a nuisance, and the hiring fair for servants was 'the public display of the poorest wretches of the community who were unable to find any other employment'.

No. 42 Cricklade Street. Although Cricklade Street was referred to as such from the 1600s, it was in effect a continuation of High Street – which is where its inhabitants often claimed to live. Here, descending Brock Hill, was the main road north that connected with the lane to Stratton St Margaret; a parish that Swindon was later to partly annexe. The top of Brock Hill was surely seen as High Street when an early 18th-century person of wealth, built what is now No.42, in just the right position to make an architectural statement. At one time, it was owned by Swindon's 'second' family, the Viletts. The house was built nearly half a century before the Goddards remodelled theirs, when they were certainly influenced by the Cricklade Street property.

42 Cricklade Street

The oldest, unspoiled private house façade in old Swindon, and certainly the most ornate, is 42 Cricklade Street, formerly known as The Hall.

Pevsner called it 'the best house in Swindon by far' and John Betjeman said it was 'one of the most distinguished town houses in Wiltshire'. In 1728 there were two adjoining buildings on this site; one was a dwelling and the other an unoccupied building formerly known as the White Horse inn. Evidence of this is suggested by the brick-vaulted cellars, which are more extensive than would be required by a private house. They were connected to the old town tunnels, and therefore the suggestion that they were involved in liquor smuggling and concealment is inescapable. Both buildings were demolished, and in their place The Hall was erected in 1729, either for the Harding family or else it was soon acquired by them. It may have been built by a local landowner named William Harding, or it may have passed to Robert Harding who certainly lived there before his death in 1770, after which it was acquired by the Vilett family. Built of brick with stone dressings, No. 42 is a broad, two-storey edifice of five bays, flanked by flat pilasters with Composite caps. It has an exceptionally 'busy', symmetrical façade; a riot of decorative motifs such as stepped keystones with faces, moulded dressings and cornices. The three central

The Hermitage, off Market Square, was a large, neo-Tudor, early Victorian house built by High Street chemist and druggist Charles Anthony Wheeler, who also built Rose Cottage in Drove Road. The Hermitage was clearly the product of irons in several fires, for in the 1820s, Mr Wheeler also claimed to be a printer, and by the 1840s – when he had added bookseller, stationer and cigar dealer to his list of trades – he was holding occasional cattle sales from a yard at the back of his shop. Wheeler's assistant, Francis Broome Pinnegar, eventually took over the chemist's shop and became as well-known a 19th-century worthy as had been his predecessor. The Hermitage was basically two gabled wings linked by a central core, with a roof at right angles to the gables. One side of the building was timber framed. In 1964, the Hermitage became a short-stay home for the elderly, and was eventually demolished in 1994.

bays are pedimented at roof level and the whole has a plain parapet, pierced with balusters either side of the pediment. Above the imposing ground floor entrance there is an elaborate Venetian window. Inside, its most distinguishing feature was the early 18th-century staircase with turned balusters, ascending through three levels.

Early alehouses and inns

In a 17th-century quarter sessions, the constables of the Kingsbridge hundred presented 'that in the towne of Swindon there are nine licensed Alehouses which we thinke to be to manie in a Towne where there are not 300 communicants in

Bell Inn, High Street. The legend over the door claims that this inn was established in 1515. It is said to have come about when Flemish wine and spirit merchants established a retail outlet in the town that was much patronised by the gentry of the day. Here was 'the Lapwinge', a messuage that Richard Goddard (Lord of the Manor 1644–50) conveyed to Samuel Haggard, yeoman of Swindon, in December 1649. Perhaps it was then renamed, for a document of 1666 refers to the 'signe of the Bell in Swindon'. In the early 19th century it was the town's Post Office, when Charles Rose was both innkeeper and postmaster. At that time, the post coach (which also carried passengers) left the Bell for London three times a week at 6.30am. It was also the stopping place for the passenger coach that ran between Bath and Oxford. By the 1840s the mail coaches were more frequent, and one wonders whether the postmaster personally attended the daily round-the-clock deliveries and despatches. Some time in the mid-1840s, Mr Rose and his Post Office removed to Bath Road. Frederick Edwin and James Franklin took over the Bell. For many years the inn's frontage was distinguished by a canopy that spanned the pavement from the front door.

being no thorowfare'. Documentary evidence is slight for the early years of the 18th century, but there are sufficient references to paint a reasonable picture of a town at the time, well appointed with drinking places. There are a number of reasons for this. Some were established during Swindon's days as a wool centre, and remained in business as the wool trade declined. Others came about in order to supply drovers,

Belmont Steam Brewery, Devizes Road. William Godwin's 'Belmont' was the younger of the two major breweries that developed between High Street and Devizes Road. Its origins were in a brew house behind the Bell Inn. Godwin acquired it c.1870 and it remained a family business until the late 1930s. Later it was used as a store room, fell into obscurity and dilapidation, and was for many years the haunt of tramps. The building was gutted, refurbished and opened as a nightclub in 1998. The outside walls are original, as are some of the internal supporting pillars. The brewery's original tower and chimney in brick and stone, remain a landmark in the old town.

farmers and traders at the town's markets and fairs. One or two started off associated with some other trade, notably that of baker, butcher or miller, or simply developed from being a cottage

Bowly's Brewery, High Street. All that separated the North Wilts Brewery from Godwin's were a couple of extremely long gardens. Notably, one of these which ran the whole way from High Street to Devizes Road, belonged to J.E.G. Bradford, the well-known Swindon solicitor. The brewery had its origins in a High Street alehouse that may well have existed in the 17th century. Bowly himself claimed that the business was established in 1765. The brewery's long High Street frontage, formed out of a house and commercial premises that were probably built during the first third of the 19th century, are retained in the present-day Barclays Bank building. It is distinguished by the central archway which accommodated carriages, and which now forms the main entrance to the bank. Until they were demolished in the 1980s, the lane through this archway to the brewery was lined by a row of 19th-century cottages and outhouses.

Mason's Arms. When the Mason's Arms was demolished in the early 1970s to facilitate road widening, it was the third oldest inn extant in Swindon. Some of the fabric of the building probably dated from the late 1600s, and beneath the inn there was access to a number of the brick-lined passages that connected certain old Swindon buildings. In 1830, the innkeeper was Richard Tarrant, and it is quite likely that he had been there for some considerable time. Tarrant was recorded as a freeholder in 1818, and the inn's change of name from the Coach & Horses, may have preceded that date, coinciding with the start of his incumbency. He was followed in 1841 by William and Caroline Killard. In 1863, John Washbourne of Wroughton took over. He is especially interesting because, at the time, he owned land at Wroughton which the Swindon Water Company was to buy in 1866 in order to make their reservoir. This land included two copyhold cottages, and after the purchase, the occupants were served notice to quit. At the Mason's Arms, he was succeeded in 1870 by Matthew Washbourne, who was followed by Thomas Wheeler in 1873. Arkell's Brewery bought the Mason's Arms in 1886 and it remained part of their estate for the next 83 years, before it was acquired by Swindon Borough Council for the purposes of urban redevelopment. The stables and stable yard stood on the north side of the car park, now adjacent to modern buildings facing Newport Street.

industry beer house frequented by a particularly close section of the community. Also, their number was influenced by Swindon's geographical position. The town might have been fairly insignificant in itself, but it was on a vital route between the south coast and the Cotswolds. It was in just the right position to be a welcoming watering hole both for long-distance travellers and coach horses (particularly after they had ascended the gradient into the town).

In this respect, the first welcome sight – certainly in the early years of the 18th century – was the White Horse inn just as the hill flattened out into Cricklade Street, with the Dog almost opposite. On the east side of High Street there was the Crown (now the Goddard Arms) and almost opposite was the Shoulder of Mutton. Further along Wood Street, on the south side, was the Red Lion. The Angel was next door to the Crown, followed almost immediately by the Bull. Opposite stood the King's Head (renamed King of Prussia after Waterloo), almost next to the Ram, a few doors away from the Lapwing (now the Bell), then the Bear. Almost opposite the latter was the Coach and Horses, renamed the Mason's Arms in the early years of the 19th century. On the north-east corner of Newport Street there was the Royal Oak (extant), close by the George, with the White Hart (later renamed the Bull) further to the west on the south side. As far as it is possible to tell from known documents, as many as 15 licensed houses, most open at any one time, were in existence during the first few decades of the 1700s. It is said that by 1800 'there were more public houses in Swindon than any other business', and they were only obliged to remain closed for one hour in 24. Little notice was taken of the licensing laws.

The King's Head

One of the worst acts of architectural vandalism in the history of Swindon occurred in 1981, when the High Street building that was formerly the King's Head/King of Prussia inn was destroyed and subsequently redeveloped into offices. The building itself very likely originated as a cottage or

two in the 16th century, or otherwise utilised materials of that period in some later reconstruction. When it was pulled down, it was the only building of its age and type in the town. Its front rooms, front cellars, tiled roof and stone façade with a flat string moulding were built early in the 17th century. Internally, there were chamfered beams with decorative stops, and partitioning with characteristic vertical overlap put up in both the 17th and 18th centuries. The frontage occupied 33ft of roadway, with a run of market traders' pitching posts and poles which could be rented, along its length. Early in the 18th century, a large, separate assembly room or ballroom was built at the back, next to a considerable quantity of stabling. The assembly room had a frieze of egg and dart moulding with merman brackets below the plaster moulding. A crest over the two doors showed a hand with a heart in its centre and a ribbon at the base; the whole motif surrounded by olive branches. The front rooms were used as the alehouse and were well patronised by the Lords of the Manor of Swindon and visiting gentry.

This was without doubt a very important hostelry. During the 18th century, two cellars were built behind the earlier ones and were used for storing beer and wine respectively. The assembly room was altered in the 19th century, reflecting its importance, particularly on market days, during fairs and feasts and as a place of entertainment. It also developed a reputation as a venue for prostitutes, the girls doing business in rooms gained by stairs inside the assembly room. A small window was inserted in the outside wall so that a lookout could be kept in case the constable appeared. Mary Ellison was the landlady in 1832. The 'King' was also famed for the frequency of the brawls that took place there.

So valuable was this establishment to the town's trade that, in the mid-1860s, the Swindon Central

Market Company wanted to convert it into a corn exchange. The owner, John Harding Sheppard (who lived just a few doors away until his death in 1868 at the age of 90), refused. The inn closed in 1880, and the building was taken over by the Smith family of butchers. It remained their property for nearly a century. In 1977, it was bought by the Midland Bank, and subsequently planning permission was given for the demolition of the back of the building and redevelopment as offices, so long as the façade was retained. Despite a large petition by Swindonians, a later application was successful for demolition of the building and redevelopment of the site as a whole.

The Goddard Arms

Before it became the Goddard Arms at some time in the second decade of the 19th century, the Crown was a small cottage alehouse, built of stone and thatched. A wooden sign swung above the doorway. As the Goddard Arms, it rapidly became the most important building in the town. It has variously been the venue for the Court Leet, the magistrate's court, county court and petty sessions, a meeting place for most of the trader groups and societies throughout the 19th century, the home of a succession of auctioneers and sales, and a place of entertainment for the townspeople. After the Great Western Railway reached Swindon, the Goddard Arms became the town's booking office, selling tickets for both open and closed carriages. The earliest known reference to the Crown is in a 25-year lease by Sir Richard Bridges, who then held the manor of West Swindon, to a man named Allworth. When the latter died, his widow married William West, who in 1581 bought the freehold of the Crown from

Goddard Arms, High Street. This was the most important hotel in the old town for much of the 19th century, when it was at the centre of many of the social and business activities. It made the news in 1914 when Frances Priscilla Hunter, employed there as a between maid, was murdered in the hotel's coal house. After the maid admitted an affair with a married man, whilst also walking out with painter and decorator Walter James White, the latter shot her twice in the head. He then waited on the arrival of Amos Church, the manager, who had heard the shots, and gave himself up.

Providence Row. This, Victory Row and Union Row were examples of many little terraces of cottages on short, very narrow streets, usually linking bigger thoroughfares.

Anthony Bridges who had acquired his late father's estate. West died in 1610, when the Crown passed to his son Thomas, upon whose death seven years later it was part of the estate inherited by his son William. Meanwhile, Thomas Goddard, the first of the family to become Lord of the Manor of Swindon, acquired his position in 1563, and it was to him that William West sold the Crown in 1621.

Not a lot is definitely known about the inn during the next 200 years. It was leased to Thomas Kibblewhite in 1633, and in 1703 to William Elton, together with the profits from fairs and markets. Several members of the Gray family held it during the 18th century, and it seems likely that c.1780, before it was renamed, the inn was rebuilt. It was valued at £18.10s in 1806; £40 in

1825, and £33 in 1832. A large assembly room was built adjoining the Goddard Arms in 1850, and was thereafter used for public balls and concerts. The inn's most famous 19th-century innkeeper was William Westmacott, who had been a Swindon saddler and harness maker since 1832, and who acquired the lease of the Goddard Arms Commercial & Posting House in 1857. Nineteen years later, it was acquired by Bowly's brewers, although true to its cottage brewing origins, it continued to advertise home brewed beer. After the railway arrived to the north of the hill, horse-drawn omnibuses left the Goddard Arms for Swindon station six times daily, charging 6d for the ride and another 6d for luggage. At the back of the inn there were pig sties and a sale yard regularly used by auctioneer William Dore, where well into the 20th century, John Maskelyne sold sheep, cattle and horses. When the Lord of Manor wanted to call people together to discuss matters of some moment in the town, he did so at the Goddard Arms. And whenever new buildings of perceived importance were opened thereabouts during the 19th century, it was invariably at the Goddard Arms that the worthies assembled, and from there that processions set out.

It is claimed that Robert Watkins, who was wrongly accused of murder in 1819, ate his last meal at the Goddard Arms, whilst waiting for the hangman to arrive from Salisbury. Then he was taken a few miles to Purton Stoke and hanged at a crossroads for the crime to which his father later confessed. The crossroads is said still to be haunted by his ghost. The writer Robert Smith Surtees also spent some time at the hotel in the 1830s before writing *Jorrocks' Jaunts and Jollities* (1838). Now it is a distinguished two-storey building that blocks the view at the end of Wood Street and marks the point where High Street and Cricklade Street meet. It is built of diaper brickwork, usually concealed by creeper, beneath a mansard roof. The front entrance to the old part is beneath an arch from the late 18th-century rebuilding, uncovered in 1955, and inscribed 'licensed to let post horses'.

Swindon in the early 1800s

The first third of the 19th century is a good point at which to take stock of Swindon and provide an overview of the town. This is because little had changed for centuries, but much was about to. Indeed, as late as 1830, a commentator was still able to describe Swindon as 'a town of two principal streets'. One assumes that this refers to High Street and Wood Street, because it was in these that most of the better buildings were to be found and the more important tradespeople had

As far as traders were concerned, Wood Street reached its peak in the 1870s. The street must have buzzed with commerce and trade, and this selected list of those who lived or worked there in the 1870s, with the numbers of their premises, shows what was then available. 1, John Hinton Pruce, hairdresser (and one-time keeper of a servants' register). 2, James Tarrant, saddler. 3, John Giles, fishmonger. 4, Henry Bond & Sons, jewellers. 5, Edwin Knapp & Co. grocers. 6, Frederick Harding, Manager of the Wilts & Dorset Bank. 7, The Cross Keys public house. 8, the Misses Beak and Kate Bullus, fancy repository. 9, Richard James Tarrant, boot and shoe maker (established 1740). 10, Frederick Dangerfield, greengrocer. 11, Richard Newman Blandford, builder, and Mrs Blandford, baby linen warehouse. 12, Edwin Robert Ing, chemist and aerated water manufacturer; John J. Shawyer, chemist and Amos Barns, solicitor. 13 (later also 11), Hubert John Deacon, jeweller and watchmaker, who claimed to have established in 1838. With reference to the GWR works, he manufactured watches which he 'warranted to keep 'hooter' time'. 14, Broom Vines, draper. 15, Great Western Photographic Company. 16, Mrs Booth and Samuel Hawson, booksellers and stationers and Richard Cook, confectioner. 17, Edward John Keylock, butcher. 18, Lewis Foss & Son, gentlemen's outfitters. 19, John Green, chemist and stamp office. 20, King's Arms Hotel and stamp office. 22, William Vaughan Edwards & Co., ironmongers, (sometime Edwards & Suter's), whose Castle Iron Works had a distinguished stone entrance corridor next to the King's Arms Hotel. 23, Mary Ann, stationer and bookseller, successor to Isaac Ann; William Wilson, outfitter and hosiery. 24, Robert Few, game dealer and poulterer. 25, Alfred Adams, boot maker; and Joseph Bishop, confectioner. 26, Edwin John Lay, watchmaker. 27, Henry Lay, confectioner, luncheon and dining rooms. 29, Abraham Coleman; James Kent, furniture dealer, and James Pruce, watchmaker. 30, Edward King, carriage works, coach builder and cycle store on the corner with Little London. 31, William Henry Read, architect, civil engineer and surveyor. 33, Edward Smith, butcher. 35, John Chandler & Son, draper.

their premises. Interestingly, Newport Street – despite having then been occupied for at least 500 years – appears not to have been significantly developed, either in terms of architecture or trade.

Bath Road, east end. This eastern part of the Sands was being called Bath Road as early as the 1850s, although was not officially designated as such. This was where Swindon's 19th-century architects were allowed to experiment on behalf of the most affluent of the retailers and public service providers. William H. Read, overseer and surveyor to the Old Swindon Local Board, the architect of so many new public buildings and the man who remodelled or rebuilt many of the older residential properties, formerly lived at No.10. The most pleasing buildings extant in Bath Road were all put up before 1845, but many impressive, architecturally designed villas of character were built between 1860 and 1880. Some of them lack taste and were more of an outward statement of their owners' affluence. As Bath Road began to fill up from the 1850s, traders started to creep along it from the Wood Street end. By the mid-1860s, there was Bainbridge's millinery and dressmaking establishment, Richard Bowly's carpet and blanket warehouse, and John Spiller's upholstery business. Certainly by 1880, Bath Road was at its residential and fashionable peak. The Post Office was still at No.11, its location since the 1840s. Residences had appeared with names like Fairview, Alexandria House, Ightham Villa, Longford Villa, Eversely, Sandown Villa and Auckland House. Miss Brown's Ladies' School was there, as were Samuel Snell's High School and William Jenkins' Sandhill House School. The solicitors William Foote and Robert Foreman lived at No.15 and No.41 respectively. Architect T.S. Lansdown lived at Fairfield House. Important and long-established tradespeople also lived there; boot and shoe repairer Richard Tarrant was at No.16, and John Toomer the coal and coke merchant was at Bella-vista.

At the lowest end of the social scale were the occupants of the town's workhouse. This was built *c.*1768, fairly close to the pest house that had preceded it at Okus by only a few years, close to the Swindon quarries. The workhouse remained until late in the 19th century.

In 1801, Swindon had a population of 1,198; it had risen to 1,742 by 1831. A valuation made in 1806 revealed 133 people in the parish who occupied houses or buildings with adjoining gardens or closes. The Poll Book of 1818 records only 35 freeholders in the parish. Of these, gentry were represented by John and Thomas Blanchard, Henry Bullock, Charles Bradford, Thomas Coventry, William Harding, Thomas Jones, Robert Large, John Osborne, James Trow and William Weeks. Henry Noad was both baker and parish clerk and the local insurance agent was Richard Strange. James Bradford and William Morse Crowdy were solicitors. The two Wood Street blacksmiths, Sadler Bristow and John Horn, were included, as were two innkeepers, William Ellison of the King of Prussia and Richard Tarrant of the Mason's Arms. Retail traders on the list included tea dealer John Butler, Thomas Lamb the linen and woollen draper, grocer James Strange, William Scotford the tailor and the two ironmongers George Lawrence and Laurence Lawrence. Traders who were also freeholders included Abraham Harris the miller, maltster William Farmer, John Shepherd who dealt in wines and spirits, and boot and shoemaker James Tarrant. Moses Goold was a painter and sculptor, Thomas Selby a bricklayer, Joseph Woodham, John Tarrant and Seymour Tarrant were all masons, and Thomas Weeks – father and son – were carpenters.

At the beginning of the century, the town was about to receive the first of two waves of 'navvies' – itinerant builders who first came to construct the Wilts & Berks Canal, and then the Great Western

Railway by another generation less than 40 years later. Some of the managers and officials of both these enterprises remained in Swindon with their families. But in 1800, there was little indication of anything that was likely to change the humdrum existence of the little town on the hill. Twenty years later, it would be recorded as having 1,580 people, and in 1831 there would be 1,742. In four decades the population of Old Swindon more than doubled, reaching 2,495 by 1841.

Travellers approaching from the north came through the Marsh, a boggy, smelly area surrounded by open fields. It was rumoured to be the source of fevers that afflicted the local inhabitants. However, the general sanitary conditions inflicted far more. Effluent from the Brockwell slaughter houses and the town's butchers shops simply ran into the roadway. Sewage drained from cesspools, overflowed into gardens, yards and streets or found its way into the wells that supplied the town's water. Theoretically, the waste drained into pits, and when the gullies were blocked it leached out, pervading the air with a foul stench. The inhabitants lived under sentence of typhoid, typhus, smallpox and infantile diarrhoea.

They also lived under the fear of fire that might destroy their thatched properties and cause personal injury. It is no accident that several insurance companies had agents in the parish. Anyone requiring the manual fire engine during the first half of the 19th century had first to organise sufficient people to manhandle it. Then they had to rush round to the police house in Devizes Road or the offices of the assistant overseer in Wood Street, where there were duplicate keys. The wooden engine itself, painted red and complete with hoses and buckets, was kept locked up at the latter's premises in Newport Street. The engine was also 'available for surrounding towns and villages, under certain stipulations'! When the Volunteer Fire Brigade was formed in 1879, the fire engine was taken to the Swindon Water Company's offices at Quarry House, The Sands. It was kept there until a permanent Swindon Fire Brigade was formed in Lansdown Road.

After 1804, the little bridge over the Wilts & Berks Canal prepared the traveller for disembarking a few minutes later. His coach may have been The Plough from Cheltenham, en route for Southampton, and scheduled to call at the Goddard Arms in High Street at midday every Monday, Wednesday and Friday. As it reached the foot of the hill, it passed a wooded area, screening quarries to the east, followed by Swindon House and then Goddard estate lands. To the west there was Eastcott Farm, roughly where Regent Circus would be built nearly a century later. The road ascending the hill was high-banked and thickly hedged, with farmland on the other side stretching to the steeply inclined roadway that linked hilltop Swindon with Eastcott Farm. By the 1850s this would be called Eastcott Lane, when the few isolated dwellings that bordered it earlier in the century had become little terraces of cottages.

Coaches struggled up Brockhill and the incredibly sharp incline before levelling out in Cricklade Street, and clattering into the stable yard of the Crown. On any Monday, the residue of the weekly market would still be about, and both the Crown, the King's Head opposite, the Bell a little further along High Street and the Coach and Horses beyond the Market Square, would be packed with dealers and market traders. The Bell did not have the Victorian frontage we see today, but was a low building with a galleried upper storey surrounding the stable yard.

Throughout the year, there were special fairs on designated Mondays for cattle, horses, sheep, pigs and sundries, when a miscellany of travelling pedlars added to the numbers in the hostelries. On days in April and September, it must have seemed to Swindon that the world had descended on their little town, for it was then that servants were hired. It is difficult to determine with any certainty how successful were the various Swindon markets in the opening years of the new century. Whilst writers tended to maintain that 'great' or 'good' markets were held here, one wonders whether this was based more on hearsay. After all, the market building and market cross had recently been removed, and by all accounts trading in the Market Square was in decline. The Portland stone quarries were not being worked to any great extent, but some of the inhabitants were employed in the brick and tile works which may have existed from the 18th century. Most of the inhabitants, however, were involved in agriculture.

In the first few years of the 19th century, Swindon gave comparatively little to the outside world, and there would seem to have been neither incentive nor need for expansion. The town's traders serviced only the day-to-day needs of its inhabitants. Swindon's gentry lived in some comfort in recently-built, plain Georgian stone houses in High Street and Wood Street. These roadways were also the main centres of retail trade. In this respect, there was little to choose between them; both thoroughfares included bakers, blacksmiths, boot and shoe makers, and carpenters. Both had inns and posting houses. Of the two, however, Wood Street was the most workaday. It was sometimes called 'Blacksmith Street' after the open forges which John Elborough and William Bristow had been operating since the 1770s. They worked amongst the thatched, labourers' cottages that lined the road, and were a magnet for the agricultural workers on cold evenings. Wood Street also housed the town's bookseller, and the Post Office that was soon to remove around the corner into High Street.

At the point where the road turned into Cricklade Street, the famous Blackford brothers had their butchers shop. The original building was put up here in the 1740s, and was rebuilt about 1845 when Robert Blackford took over a former dairy and brewhouse in High Street that had also just been rebuilt. The Blackfords leased a slaughterhouse and stabling nearby in Cricklade Street. They were responsible, it must be said, for some rather insanitary conditions when blood from the processes at their slaughterhouse found its way on to the streets of Swindon. On the opposite side of the road, the corner of Wood Street and High Street, there was a fine old, double gabled building, at least part of which was occupied by ironmonger Laurence Lawrence until the mid-1840s. This has been identified as the shop mentioned in a lease of 1712, so appears to have been a building continuously associated with trade – and in particular ironmongery – for several centuries.

Various mail coaches brought letters from London and Marlborough at 7.00am, from Wootton Bassett at 6.30 in the evening, and half an hour later from Highworth – which was the sorting office for coaches from the Midlands and the North. Mail coaches left Swindon at 7.00am for Wootton Bassett, the Midlands and the north, and 12 hours later for Marlborough.

High Street had a number of larger, gabled houses of a type still to be seen opposite the gates to the former Goddard estate, and was altogether more affluent. It also had more traders overall but the mix of these, officials such as land and tax agents, and what we would now call service industries – bankers, insurance agents, surgeons – was very similar. There was also the Crown inn, soon to be renamed the Goddard Arms. Before Swindon had a town hall, this inn was the centre for most public and legal business carried out in the town. As late as 1900, Swindon had a very

Bowmaker House, Wood Street. The appearance of Wood Street changed very considerably during the latter decades of the 19th century. Two-storey houses, some with displays in little bow windows that had grown out of front rooms, became three-storey buildings with full-width shop fronts at street level. Commerce and trade paid for stylish façades with, for the most part, restrained classical features and a gothic 'feel'. At the west end, the late Georgian Bowmaker House of four bays has escaped such conversion. When the street began to be developed as it is today, this was probably the most imposing private dwelling there. The only external alteration since it was built, involved swapping around a window with the lovely little pedimented doorway that now occupies the third bay.

different 'feel'. Anyone standing beside the Market Square and looking north along High Street would have seen rows of façades reminiscent of those in nearby Cotswold towns.

The poorest thoroughfare, Newport Street, was a real mixture. It was also known as 'Bull Street' after its notorious public house, and comprised mostly low, thatched cottages built of undressed stone, mud and lime coated in limewash and supported by rough hewn timbers. Some of these were on the sites of dwellings that went back to at least the 14th century. The walls were rarely perpendicular and the cottages were out of alignment with each other. Here in the 19th century lived Henry Noad, the parish clerk, and here too were the offices of William Morse Crowdy and Alfred Southby, at that time the town's only solicitors. These, however, were the exception. Living and working here at various times were also bakers, butchers, carpenters, coopers, cottage shopkeepers in spirits and sundries, dressmakers, grocers, ironmongers, maltsters, plumbers and glaziers, sign painters, tailors and tea dealers. Most of these trades were carried on from cottages on the south-west side of the street; those in the south-east section and most of the north side were occupied by generations of poor, agricultural workers.

Just how poor they were, came to light when redevelopment of Newport Street in the latter part of the 20th century revealed several sets of human remains in the gardens, indicating that some of the inhabitants may simply have been buried behind their cottages when they died. If the gentry patronised the establishments of Wood Street and High Street, it was the cottage industries and front room shops of Newport Street that satisfied the less affluent townspeople. The beginning of Marlborough Road out of the old town, was marked by a thatched inn, the Red Lion, that stood at right angles to the thoroughfare. This hostelry was renamed the Bell and Mutton by 1830 when George Austin was landlord, and 'Shoulder of' was added to the name sometime during the 1840s.

19th-century expansion

Old Swindon expanded modestly during the first half of the 19th century. Devizes Road was almost

uninhabited except for a few workmen's cottages, before the Britannia Place dwellings were built off of it from 1818. Thereafter, houses began to creep along the old trackway; one notable and extant example on the east side being Canford House with its wrought iron porch. Built during the 1830s, this was the sometime police house of Supt. Henry Haynes, and held the occasional wrongdoer

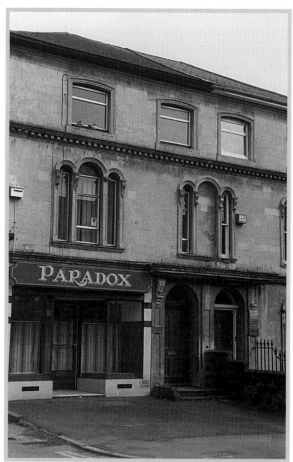

Devizes Road was one of the later roads to be built up in the old town. This originally comprised Shortedge or Short Hedge in its southern part where the road left the old town towards Wroughton. The rest of Devizes Road was called Horsefair or Horsefair Street until about 1853. During the 18th and early 19th centuries, sales of horses were held here, and the 'short hedge' was the one they faced whilst waiting for inspection, with their back legs in the roadway. Not unsurprisingly, blacksmith Thomas Greenaway lived here by the 1840s, and during the next few years he was joined by carpenter Thomas Weeks. Apart from the police house, there was very little residential accommodation here until midway through the 19th century. The most distinguished building extant is an Italianate-style terrace that was put up on the eastern side.

Tritton House, Bath Road. Built *c*.1835 as a gentleman's residence, and at one time named Grafton Cottage, No.14 Bath Road is distinguished as being detached from the nearby terrace of three town houses of similar date. It is not as grand as the stone houses that were to be put up in Bath Road over the next decade, and was designed in brick and stone by a much lighter hand. It is distinguished by its interesting fanlight, the lunette attic lights and wrought iron, canopied porch. The later extension is also 19th-century. Later in the same century it was owned by Henry Smith; the partner in the firm of auctioneers Dore, Smith & Radway, which office he took up in 1876, the year before the well-liked William Dore died, aged 65. The building had been used as offices for some time when it was acquired by the Swindon Conservative Association in 1973, which has since sub-let parts of it to other companies. It is named Tritton House after Sir G.E. Tritton who twice fought the seat unsuccessfully for the Conservatives in the early 1950s.

Bath Road Terrace. This pretty little terrace was put up in the mid-1830s, and must have been a stark contrast to the utilitarian cottage architecture of the old town. Swindon's builders seem to have had a Bath fixation. In 1845, hardly ten years after this terrace was built, architect and builder Thomas Rose, who also kept the Post Office in High Street, leased a plot of land at the northern end of Devizes Road for building. The result was a terrace of nine substantial town houses named Bath Buildings, and an arrangement of smaller dwellings, Bath Cottages, built around three sides of a yard at the rear. Around the corner in Bath Road was Bath Terrace, distinguished in the 1860s at street level by the long run of Spiller's furniture, upholstery and cabinet manufactory. Bath Buildings and Bath Terrace remain, although their façades are substantially altered.

by means of metal rings in the walls of the cellar. The first new road to go in outside the main town was also being developed by the early 1830s; small stone houses were built in Prospect, close to the northern end of Victoria Street. These were put up along the track which, before the northern

expansion of the latter, was a principal route off the hill. Almost immediately, George Nourse opened his school for young gentlemen there.

For the first three decades, Wood Street retained much of its cottage architecture; a mixture of labourers' thatched dwellings, blacksmiths' forges and early on, a windmill. But here too, there were changes; larger houses took the place of some of the cottages at the High Street end, and the gentry and professional people moved in. Suddenly the eastern end of The Sands, to be designated Bath Road in 1850, became popular. Here was virgin land, separated from the rough and tumble of the old town, and ripe for colonisation by fashionable middle-class society. A number of buildings were put up on the north side in the 1830s and 1840s, taking advantage of the fine views where the north-western edge of the hill plunged into the lowlands, with the glistening ribbon of the Wilts & Berks Canal in the distance.

Britannia Inn, Devizes Road. By the 1840s, only a handful of cottages lined the north side of Britannia Place, close to Devizes Road. They were about 30 years old, and had been built on a lane that, at the time, cut into long gardens running from the rear of High Street properties. In the late 1840s, Britannia Place was given a dog-leg extension beside a site that was to become William Butler's second Swindon brewery, later the Belmont, to which it also provided access. Here was built a residential terrace of small, red brick houses with front and back gardens. A little community was establishing along Britannia Place when, also in the late 1840s, the Britannia alehouse opened, kept by Richard Stagg, on the corner with Devizes Road. By 1858, there were 23 houses in Britannia Place and a rather grander dwelling called 'Britannia Cottage'. They all took water from a single supply known as the 'Britannia Pump' which was on private land owned by Charles Anthony Wheeler and to which he allowed free public access. It was not the Belmont, but Richard Bowly's North Wilts Brewery that bought the Britannia in 1870. They gave it the name 'The Fountain', which it was to retain for more than 120 years. It has gone down in history as providing the dressing rooms for Swindon Town Football Club and

their opposition when they played matches at the Croft. The pub has seen several changes of name; in this photograph it was the Piper's Arms.

The change of name seemed to give it instant credibility, and over the next three decades a number of fine villas were built along its length. It was said to be 'a very healthy and pleasant locality, destined to become the resort of more wealthy inhabitants'.

Most notable of Bath Road's larger residences was Apsley House, which has been the Swindon

Prospect Place. A picturesque row of gabled cottages, in rough Swindon stone with Bath stone dressings, and corridors with depressed arches; all rather reminiscent of the railway village cottages. This lane was laid out in the 1830s.

Apsley House and Gallery, Bath Road. For a couple of decades at Apsley House the Swindon museum was a voluntary concern with an honorary curator, C.H. Gore, who had been in charge of the collection since it was brought together in 1920. When he died in 1951, it came under the control of Harold Jolliffe who was designated Borough Librarian & Curator, on behalf of the Swindon Borough Council's Libraries, Museums & Arts Committee. The most nationally famous of the town's curators was Neil (later Sir Neil) Cossons. He was followed by the ebullient John Woodward, who did much for archaeological research in the area. In 1964, a linked art gallery was added to the museum, above shops on part of the corner site with Victoria Road, where once had stood the Congregational Church of 1866.

Museum since 1930. Prior to that, the collection was housed in a chapel that the Unitarians built in Regent Circus, which was later bought by the Roman Catholics and became empty when the latter removed to their church in Groundwell Road. Apsley House is a Georgian residence, built c.1830 of Bath stone with the added pretentious flourish of a Doric portico. An early occupant was the Old Town surgeon Charles James Fox Axford. He had premises variously in Wood Street, High Street and Prospect Place. Axford eventually removed to New Swindon and Apsley House was taken over by a colleague, Frederick Henry Morris. In 1862, the house passed into trade, acquired by coal and coke merchant Richard Tarrant who already had premises nearby and a depot at the New Swindon station. Exactly the same was true of the Tarrant brothers' great rival John Toomer, who also dealt in lime, salt and hay. He had established a wharf at Swindon station in

Croft House, the Croft. One of Swindon's most successful businesses was the department store that Levi Lapper Morse (1853–1913) established in Regent Street in the 1870s. Morse's was eventually taken over by his son William Ewart. Both men were sometime MPs and Mayors of the town; Levi being the second to hold office after the Borough was created, and his son at the outbreak of hostilities in 1914. The family were ardent Primitive Methodists who lived at Croft House. This was a huge, four-square house, built in the 1840s, with bay windows to both storeys, and in extensive grounds. The family acquired it in 1896. The imposing exterior suggested a very lavish interior, and this was certainly the case, proving just how successful was the business. Both father and son were benefactors in the community. The grounds at Croft House included sweeping beds, borders and flower gardens. They were frequently used for fêtes and other social gatherings, and a whole series of Primitive Methodist conventions.

1849, bought Apsley House as a family residence in 1870, and took over Tarrant's Bath Road depot. It was here that he really expanded the business, supplying all manner of commodities. John Toomer's corn store, a four-storey brick building that he put up in the 19th century, on the site of two old cottages where Market Square meets High Street, is still there. Although it is now offices, this building, which once had cheese lofts on the second floor, is the most tangible reminder of Swindon's agricultural past. Apsley House was variously extended, although part of the extension was demolished in 1964 to accommodate the adjacent Swindon Art Gallery.

Soon after Apsley House was built, so too was a terrace of three, two-storey, three-bay, red brick houses; put up immediately to the west, c.1835. They are distinguished by their lunette attic windows and openwork wrought iron porches with lead canopies. These are coeval with the detached house next door that shares many of their characteristics. At the end of the 1830s, this group would have formed the extent of the town's encroachment on The Sands. Today, they are offices. In about 1840, a new terrace was built opposite Apsley house, and it would not be long

before several were converted to shops at street level. It was in this decade that Swindon's western expansion began in earnest, and Bath Road became the canvas on which architects of the day created fine houses for people of means. Chronologically,

Royal Oak Inn, Devizes Road. These premises were made out of cottages on the corner of Newport Street and Devizes Road at some time in the 1840s. It seems an odd decision, since at the time there were no buildings to speak of in Devizes Road and, but for two large residences, hardly any immediate habitation on the road to the south. Anyone travelling through the town would already have had the opportunity to stop at several public houses, so at best – at least initially – it could claim to be the first of its kind at Swindon for people entering along the Wroughton road. Even Newport Street at the time had at least three public houses operating in it. Inexplicable though it seems, there must have been a reasonable trade at this apparently barren spot, for within a few years it had been joined by the Plough, and both are still in existence.

it began with the modest, three-bay house, built at right angles to the road *c.*1840, that now houses Bartlett Brothers. On the opposite side of the road, an exceptionally grand residence, Kode House, went up in the middle of the decade. Then an Italianate-style villa with a central tower appeared further along The Sands. This was Kingshill House, a private residence. In the 1860s, a terrace of narrow, three-storey houses was built adjacent to the Bath Terrace shops. Victoria Road, the virtual dead end that for centuries had petered out into a footpath, was not sufficiently built up to be so designated until 1848.

There was a little thatched beer house at the beginning of Marlborough Road (Lower Town) in the early 1800s; this was to become the Bell and Shoulder of Mutton. When it was remodelled in 1895 by the Swindon & North Wilts Brewery, it became one of the nicest 19th-century façades to be put up in the old town. This work produced a

Kode House, one of the early villas to be built when development started towards The Sands. This one is plain, solid and conservative; but is nicely proportioned and has some interesting features. There are flat Doric pilasters beneath a plain entablature around the doorway, moulded window architraves (hipped on the ground floor windows), and all sills are on paired brackets. The stages are separated by a wide, flat string course above equally flat end pilasters with just the hint of capitals. These mimic the pillars around the doorway. Above the string course, these decorative end stops become quoins; the architect clearly resisting the temptation to over-embellish the façade with a second tier of pilasters. As fashionable tradespeople began to design residences for Bath Road, the houses became bigger, bolder and more ornate.

solid brick building of four bays, opening on to the main road. It had stone dressings, a whole range of decorative motifs and mouldings, and an almost continuous string course, incorporating the hood mouldings over the windows with their decorative keystones and circular labels. The entire central section of the west front was accentuated by strong sets of flanking pilasters at both ground floor and first floor levels, topped by finials. Behind the passage at the side of the inn there was considerable stabling.

Octagonal chapels

The Noad family (variously Node, Noode and Noade) was certainly in Swindon at the beginning of the 17th century, when one Nicholas Noad was parish clerk. It was an office that became quite a family affair, the long-time holder during the first part of the 19th century being Henry Noad, otherwise a baker of Newport Street. But it was William Noad, who lived in a house on the Coate road, who obtained the licence that allowed Methodism to gain a foothold through the services held on his premises. Inevitably, this led to a purpose-built chapel. The inhabitants of Newport Street probably viewed the little two-storey Independent Chapel and adjacent schoolroom that was put up in their midst in 1803, as something of a revolution in architecture. It had a tiled roof in a road of thatch; on its front was a hipped pediment above a circular window with a round-headed doorway beneath and round-headed windows on each of the sides. The first minister was Revd George Mantell who stayed there for nearly 30 years. In 1813, the Methodists put up a chapel just off the Market Square, behind a row of little cottages. In 1862, they built an extraordinary chapel with an octagonal core on the same site, then behind the Corn Exchange. The central section had a steeply pitched roof,

Congregational Church, Bath Road. When Revd G.J. Pillgrem and his congregation decided to remove from the independent chapel that had been established in Newport Street in 1805, they chose a prime site on the corner of Victoria Street and Bath Road, and commissioned a building that was to become a dominant landmark. Architect William Jervis Stent of Warminster, submitted an elaborate Lombardic-style, neo-Romanesque design. John Ponton of Warminster and Swindon's John Phillips were retained as the builders. (Stent, and Ponton whose father Joseph was a stonemason, also collaborated on Non-conformist buildings in Warminster.) The Bath Road front was 48ft wide, and the sides were 120ft long, including the school and vestry entrances to the east. The south front was dominated by a wheel window above the recessed porch, and the corner of the building was set off by a well-proportioned, three-stage tower. Like the porch, all windows and doorways were round-headed and recessed; the latter with pillars and Corinthian capitals. Each stage of the 56ft tower was treated differently.

Overall, it was probably the most attractive building most of the people in Swindon had ever seen. Internally, it was arranged as a hall with a central aisle, and a gallery at the south end – in all 545 seats. The intention was to add side galleries as the congregation increased, and a separate 40ft-high tower over the side entrances. This, however, was to remain a gabled roof. The cost of the building, furniture and fittings was a few pence short of £3,569. The building was opened at the beginning of July 1866, services having been conducted for a while previously in the schoolroom. It was almost two years later that the costs, which were wholly defrayed by public subscription, were finally accounted for. The Congregationalists decided that there would be only visiting pastors for six months, although Revd J.H. Snell made himself regularly available during the interim and took on the post permanently from the beginning of 1867. In 1868, the church was registered for solemnising marriages. The building was demolished in 1949.

topped by a little spire; otherwise the building was a succession of gabled projections. Eighteen years after they moved in, the Methodists decamped to another purpose-built chapel in Bath Road, leaving the octagon in the hands of the Salvation Army. Later it became a stable, a garage and a general store before being demolished in 1937. The Independents, later Congregationalists,

Education in the old town

In 1764, a cottage was taken over in Newport Street, and a free church school established there for 20 boys and five girls, funded by voluntary contributions and overseen by a board of trustees. Thomas Barrett was installed as its live-in master, for the premises also comprised living accommodation and a garden. Barrett taught reading, writing, arithmetic, and the principles of the Church of England; languages other than English and any form of science were inadmissible. A couple of decades into the 19th century, the school had 40 pupils. Meanwhile, the National School Society had been formed in 1811, and in 1833 it was given joint responsibility for

Methodist Church, Bath Road. When it was opened in 1879, the Bath Road Methodist Church made a fine statement in an area of affluent villas, on a roadway that was still considered to be 'an approach to the town'. Designed by Bromilow & Chears of Liverpool, to seat 600 people, it was built by Swindon's Thomas Barrett. Here was a heady mixture of neo-Romanesque architecture, a touch of Early English, and a measure of Victorian Gothic. It was paid for, in part, by public subscriptions, and in part by donations from the town's worthies. These included the GWR's Joseph Armstrong and Old Town grocer Philip Hawe Mason. (The former had been instrumental in negotiations for the New Swindon Methodists to take over the company's one-time lodging house in High Street.) A remarkable factor about Methodism in Swindon is that it took hold, initially in a fairly clandestine way, through prayer meetings in the isolated cottages of very ordinary people. It quickly burgeoned into something that appealed to people in high office in the town, and influential professional and tradespeople. Their names appear time and again on the committees and boards that formed the backbone of 19th-century Swindon's social and economic existence.

King William Street Schools were built in 1871, at a cost of £2,600. Arthur Stote, who lived adjoining the schools at No.20, was in charge of the boys. By the mid-1870s, he had three pupil teachers to help him with 200 of them; Mrs Artree and two pupil teachers looked after 150 girls, and Miss Horley and two pupil teachers managed 140 infants. Two classrooms were allocated to the boys, two for the girls, and one room for the infants. There were also morning and afternoon Sunday schools when 350 pupils attended. An 1878 report on the examination results gives an interesting insight into what was taught. 'A large proportion of boys were examined in grammar and geography; 26 of the elder boys passed successfully in mechanics and some were examined in Euclid, Algebra and Literature. The girls' special subjects were Geography and Needlework.' By this time Mr Stote had taken an assistant, W.H. Adams; a Miss Saxby and an extra pupil teacher swelled the number of tutors for the girls, and a Miss McRea had been appointed to help the infants' teacher. There were by then 340 boys in the schools, 200 girls and 260 infants. The Sunday school attendance had dropped to 290, but Tuesday evening Bible classes had been added for young women.

moved to Victoria Street in 1866, and in 1939 to Immanuel Church in Upham Road. In 1969, the Ecumenical Parish of Swindon Old Town was formed.

administering Parliamentary grants for providing school buildings throughout the country. Swindon had seen a rash of dame schools in the early years of the century, and others that operated on the principle of learning and earning side-by-side. Some of these establishments were funded by philanthropic individuals and others were simply fee-paying.

The year 1833 was also when central government began to grant-aid certain schools for the first time. 1835 saw the beginnings of a Non-conformist school for girls in Swindon. In the same year, the free school cottage was demolished to make way for Swindon's National School of 1836. This fine, stone building was distinguished by the dated name plate inscribed in its stonework. Thirty five years later, its pupils were transferred to Revd Henry George Bailey's newly-built church school in King William Street. In 1877, the Swindon School Board was formed of seven local worthies. These were Revd H.G. Bailey, James Holden (manager of the GWR's Carriage Works), Joseph Lambert (Congregational minister), Philip Hawe Mason (grocer), William Morris (newspaper proprietor), William Brewer Wearing (bank manager) and Richard Lewis White (chief accountant at the GWR). Although the National School building became, in 1909, the Parish Church Men's Club, it continued to be a landmark in Newport Street until it was demolished in

1962. Six years later, the name plate was renovated and installed on its original site, by that time the forecourt of a petrol station.

There was a quite considerable interest in education in Swindon, after the model of the original free school. William Morris recorded that,

The National School. Particularly in rural districts or amongst predominantly agricultural communities as was Swindon until the 19th century, schooling competed with work for children's time. Education was only really successfully undertaken by the moneyed classes, who in their turn often felt that it was unwise to try and educate the poor of any age. Sunday schools were the first to be established, as a means of educating lots of children on their otherwise free day of the week. This is why, as religious denominations established in Swindon, they invariably opened adjacent schoolrooms. The 1700s also saw charity schools being set up, and the often questionable dame schools. The emphasis was usually on religious matters, and such other courses of instruction in which the tutors were reasonably competent. Swindon's National School came about under the Church of England's scheme.

early in the 19th century, a school was set up in a house in Marlborough Road, and George Nourse's Classical & Commercial School for Young Gentlemen occupied a small, thatched cottage in Newport Street. By 1830, Nourse had removed to Prospect Place where his premises were being advertised as a gents' boarding and day school. Girls were being provided for by Ann Batt from a house in Wood Street, and Martha Large who had taken over the Newport Street cottage. By the mid-1800s, most of the main streets in Swindon had at least one schoolroom. Martha Jefferies ran the Ladies' School in High Street, and George's wife Catherine Nourse added a ladies' school to his school for boys in Prospect Place.

The Marlborough Road premises had also been split, with James Steger looking after the boys, and the girls in the charge of his wife Emma. Later in the century, she was to take charge in Prospect Place. The Wood Street premises continued, now run by Louisa Haines. In Victoria Street, Martha Tanner had the Ladies' Boarding School, whilst a ladies' day school was also provided by the Misses Ann and Jane Smith. By 1864, there were only three public schools in the town; a Wesleyan day school, the National School in Newport Street and an infants' school in Victoria Street. The following year, a Wesleyan school opened in The Planks. Privately, the Misses Cowell looked after the ladies' school in Prospect Place and Mrs Fentiman the young gentlemen's department. The elderly George Nourse now had his 'academy' in the school premises in Victoria Street, where his daughter looked after the ladies.

One might have thought that the arrival of the King William Street Schools in 1870 would have lessened the need for private education, but not so. Continuing to thrive in Old Swindon were the Middle Class Boys' School, Mr Snell's Classical & Commercial School, the Alexandria House Young Ladies' School, two private preparatory schools

for little boys, and in Victoria Street both Grosvenor House School and the Middle Class Girls' Collegiate School. 1870 was also the year of the Elementary Education Act that made school attendance mandatory, and imposed a duty on parents of children aged between five and 14. Seven years later, a School Board was formed to cover both Old and New Swindon, and opened its first school at Gorse Hill the following year. In 1880, the Board opened Gilberts Hill Infants School and Queenstown Infants School, which were built on the eastern and western fringes that linked the two towns.

The business of banking

Today, Lloyds TSB in High Street occupies some of Swindon's finest 19th-century buildings. The story of banking in Swindon began in the early 1800s in small, unprepossessing buildings here, on either side of the main gates to the Goddard estate. James Strange was a draper and mercer who occupied two cottages where now stands the most southerly of the present Lloyds building. Across the estate entrance there was an alehouse in 1800, then Richard Strange's grocers establishment. Both of these were later to become part of Mason's general provisions store. The Strange brothers established themselves as coal merchants on the Wilts & Berks Canal from the moment it arrived. An elder brother, Thomas, was churchwarden, coal factor and salt merchant who also worked out of the Swindon wharf. At this time, the nearest banks were in Marlborough and Devizes, and one may reasonably assume that the constant journeys thither by the busy Strange brothers became a source of irritation and the catalyst for change.

In 1807, Richard and James leased part of the house, on the northern part of the present Lloyds site, owned by churchwarden Thomas Coventry

Lloyds Bank, High Street. The fine building here was once two; the Capital & Counties Bank to the north and the County of Gloucester Bank to the south, separated by an alleyway. Diagonally across from them, in Wood Street, was the Wilts & Dorset Bank.

and which had been lived in by his family since the 17th century. At the time of the lease to the Strange brothers, this building was occupied by Joseph Gay, and used by himself and his brother John for their practice as surgeons. Eventually John (who kept five horses for his business) moved to Bath Road and Joseph to the corner of Wood Street and Cricklade Street, where he occupied a former butcher's shop which was also to become a bank. It is said that on this site he grew a small cottage garden, fertilised by the product of his outdoor blood letting activities. Another small cottage on the High Street site was occupied by a hairdresser and tobacconist named John Humphries.

The Strange brothers now occupied much of the north-east half of High Street, and it was here

in 1807 that with two others they established their bank – Strange, Garrett, Strange & Cook. The cumbersome SGS & C became James & Richard Strange & Co., and in 1826 when James died, Thomas took over his drapery business. The bank became Thomas & Richard Strange & Co., and the brothers continued a trade as coal and salt merchants on the canal.

In 1818, a 'Savings Bank' was opened in opposition, in Victoria Street. Its president was the Earl of Shaftesbury but, unlike most establishments of the time that drew officers from well-known tradespeople, it comprised for the most part, the gentry of the town. A transcript on parchment of the 'announced Rules and Regulations of the Swindon Savings Bank' was lodged with James Swayne, Deputy Clerk of the

The Wilts & Dorset bank building was erected in 1884, on a site that had been occupied at various times during the 19th century by a butcher, a boot and shoe maker, and a surgeon. Of brick, with heavy stone dressings, it made an imposing beginning to the street. The decorative motifs are all on the rounded corner entrance elevation. These begin at street level with flat, fluted pilasters and a decorated architrave surrounding the doorway, and a moulded, open ogee pediment above, decorated with a garland. The central window has a segmental, shell pediment, and the flanking windows each have swags and drop tails.

High Street, Limmex Corner c.1900. Samuel Joseph Limmex was a typical 19th-century, hands-on ironmonger who, when not so employed, surveyed his empire from a high stool behind a high desk in the little corner office. In this twin-gabled house of c.1708 Laurence Lawrence and his family lived during the first half of the 19th century, and from here he carried on an ironmongery business. At some point, the business expanded into two adjacent, small cottages in Wood Street. Lawrence was succeeded c.1845 by Edward Page, his family and live-in shopman, and then by James Wise who, in 1861, was described as ironmonger and tinplate maker. Joseph Walter, the last owner to live on the premises, continued the business until Limmex took over in 1881. This owner lived in fashionable Prospect Place. The wide range of goods that was daily displayed outside the shop, was otherwise kept in the cellar and brought up at the beginning of each day's trading. Over the years, there were considerable changes to the façade of Limmex's emporium, the earliest being his own fairly large scale reconstruction works in 1884-5. The cottages were rebuilt to the three-storey height of the High Street premises; the gables were taken down and the whole frontage remodelled, given new second and third-storey windows and a whole sweep of shop frontages at street level. Few people realise that only those sections of the roof that could be seen from the street were tiled; the rest was sheeted in tin. Behind the shop was the slaughterhouse of Smith the butcher who occupied the adjacent building, formerly the King of Prussia inn. Close by this was Limmex's tin smithy; an upstairs room where he made galvanised tin items – amongst them benches, fireplaces, bedsteads and cattle drinking troughs – which were beaten out over an old tree stump in the back yard. S.J. Limmex died in 1947, and as his only son had predeceased him, the business passed to his two daughters. Despite changes to the rest of the fabric, Limmex retained its earliest projecting shop front throughout its occupancy. From 1975 until it closed in the late 1990s, the business was run by Roy Stevens and his staff. The closure of Limmex was a great loss to Swindon's retail trade. This was the last shop in which one could purchase a single unit of some insignificant item that logic suggested had not been made for at least half a century, and be respectfully served by assistants of a 'certain age' who knew exactly what one was talking about!

Peace of the County of Wiltshire. He appended the interesting comment that it had been done 'in pursuance of the provisions of an Act of Parliament passed in the last session to Encourage the Establishment of Banks for Savings in England'. Moses Goold was the first accountant-in-residence, and this business eventually closed in 1895. Meanwhile, in 1835, the Wilts & Dorset Banking Company opened a one-room office in William Scotford's High Street tailor's shop (the Misses Harriett and Maria Scotford were milliners in the same building). This closed down after a very short period. Almost immediately, the North Wilts Banking Company seized the opportunity to fill its place, and in 1836 established itself in part of a little Wood Street house belonging to Henry Tarrant. The Tarrant family at the time were variously maltsters, boot and shoe makers and stonemasons. The bank remained in Wood Street for nine years.

In 1842, the Strange brothers' bank was taken over by the County of Gloucester Banking Company, which allowed the former principals to continue as managers. Four years later, Thomas Coventry sold his old family home to Thomas Strange. Thomas Barrett of Newport Street (builder, carpenter, appraiser and undertaker) was asked by the County of Gloucester Banking Company to rebuild the main bank building. In 1845, the North Wilts moved next door. For a while, it appears to have been run by William Morse Crowdy and Alfred Southby Crowdy, solicitors who lived in Newport Street but had their offices in High Street. The Wilts & Dorset Banking Company re-appeared in Swindon in 1876, buying surgeon John Gay's cottage in Wood Street and the low, three-storey building on the corner with Cricklade Street that housed Richard Tarrant's bootmaker's shop at street level. The bank rebuilt these premises and opened their grand offices in 1885. Six years earlier, the North Wilts became the Hampshire & North Wilts Banking Co., then the Capital & Counties Bank in the following year. Lloyds took over the County of Gloucester Bank in 1897. They also took over the Wilts & Gloucester Bank in 1915 and the Capital & Counties Bank three years later – although the latter continued to trade under its own name until 1927. Some of Swindon's most influential late Georgians and Victorians were associated with these banking enterprises.

Of beverages and light

The Swindon markets revived during the early years of the 19th century, giving rise to the 'candle and lantern' market for cattle and the 'gin and water' sale of corn. The former took place each month in High Street and frequently overflowed into Wood Street and Cricklade Street. Butchers and dealers arrived on a Sunday and put up at the

King of Prussia, the Mason's Arms or the Crown. At 3am next morning, cattle were lined up on each side of the street with their back legs in the roadway. The animals were inspected by the light of candles and lanterns, business was transacted, and the whole market was over by breakfast. The corn sales took place within the hostelries, where farmers with small samples of corn in their pockets attempted to make deals over a pipe and a glass. They frequently went from inn to inn until a satisfactory deal was struck. Eventually a 'pitched market' for corn was decided upon, the sacks being rested against posts and rails set up for that purpose in the marketplace. Corn continued to be sold in this way until 1866.

The later Old Swindon markets

A William Dore began selling cattle in Swindon about 1780; his son, also William, followed in 1795 and his son – William again – in the early 1840s. The latter's company, Dore & Fidel was well established as a seller of livestock by 1845. About 1865, William Dore III (1812–1877) built a yard just below Christ Church, on land belonging to The Swindon Market Company, where he held cattle sales for six years. Meanwhile, a Swindon Chamber of Agriculture was formed in 1866 to try and find a permanent site away from the public roads. In 1871, Thomas Hooper Deacon opened Deacon & Liddiard's Vale of White Horse & Carriage Repository from his extensive premises opposite the Market Square. He sold English and foreign horses, had stabling for up to 120 of them, standings for 50 carriages and a paddock. James Radway held cart horse shows there from 1889, when the premises had been substantially extended.

Land came up for sale in Marlborough Road, Lower Town, where William Dore built an enclosed sale ground with sale ring, clerk's office,

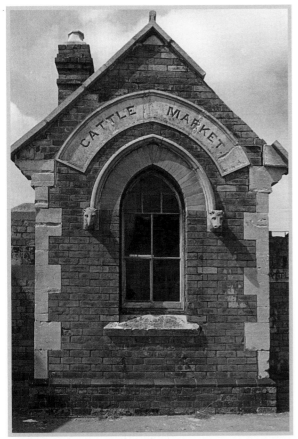

Market gatehouse, Marlborough Road. This fine building fronted one of the two entrances to Swindon Cattle Market, which occupied a large area between Marlborough Road and the Old Swindon station of the Midland & South West Junction Railway. The gatehouse was built of brick with stone quoins and dressings, and a hood moulding that ended in a sheep's head and a cow's head over the little pointed windows. It was demolished in 1970. The north-east section of the market had formerly been William Dore's cattle sale yard. The premises included a corn hall, numerous sale pens both in the open and under cover, miscellaneous outbuildings and offices.

auctioneer's rostrum and pens for 1,500 sheep, 200 head of cattle and up to 500 pigs. This was opened in 1873, and the firm of Dore, Smith & Radway ran the business after William's death. Within a few years, Ambrose Lethbridge Goddard provided an adjacent site in order to get the old cattle markets off the streets. William Read was responsible for planning the site and George Wiltshire was contracted to build it. He made pens for around 1,500 animals, with coops constructed of cast iron standards with galvanised

iron rods, supplied by William Affleck of the Prospect Iron Works. W.E. Morris, the Old Swindon surveyor, was responsible for the hard flooring, and the Swindon Water Company provided water mains, hydrants and portable watering stands. Direct access was provided to the

These two cottages on Marlborough Road were built in the early 1800s, at a time when there were very few dwellings on the turnpiked Coate road, out of Swindon and over the downs to Marlborough. One of the most interesting was the gabled Goddard estate Lodge House (demolished 1965) on the corner with Mill Lane. Before the first bank was set up in Swindon, Marlborough was the main destination for tradespeople who wanted to deposit their money. By the mid-1850s, the section of this road nearest to Swindon was called Lower Town, beginning more or less at the Bell and Shoulder of Mutton, then kept by Martha Austin. In this section, at the time, could be found James and Emma Steger who had schools for boys and young ladies respectively, Charles Smith the beer retailer, boot and shoe maker James Richard Tarrant and coach builder George Smith. Then, it was a mixture of little thatched cottages, and a hotchpotch of larger 18th and 19th-century buildings crowding in on the road. In 1867, land was leased here to Richard Tarrant, coal merchant. The road then ran south, becoming Marlborough Lane, which was later partly lost to the Midland & South West Junction Railway. It now exists only between Evelyn Street and the Pipers roundabout, before joining Marlborough Road proper. By the 1870s, this whole road was being called Marlborough Road. When the former turnpike house became available in 1876, it was leased as a residential cottage to George Saunders and, on the hill, the wine merchants Frederick John Brown and Alfred Plummer acquired a house, cottage and stable for their business. In the early years of the 20th century, Lord of the Manor, Fitzroy Pleydell Goddard regularly leased lands held by him, off Marlborough Lane and Marlborough Road, between Swindon and Coate. Notably, several members of the Button family of nurserymen acquired a number of acres of arable land from him, as did greengrocer George Davis at Coate. In 1920, land with stables in Marlborough Road was given over to the Ministry of Agriculture & Fisheries, for training disabled servicemen.

adjacent Midland & South West Junction Railway, of which Goddard was a director. There were separate entrances for pigs, sheep, horses and cattle, and a distinctive brick and stone collector's office was built on Marlborough Road. Goddard's yard opened in 1887.

Over the next few decades, sections of both these yards changed hands fairly frequently through complicated leasing arrangements. The name of Dore was retained in one of them until 1920. In 1949, the two adjacent yards were amalgamated under Amalgamated Livestock Auctioneers; several companies that already had interests in the site. The cattle sale yard remained in business until the late 1980s.

The Quarries

Despite its long association with agriculture, and centuries of livestock fairs and markets, Swindon's economy from the mid-17th century to the end of the 18th century was largely built on its Purbeck stone quarries. The deposits were just a few feet underground, and it seems likely that stone was used variously from the time of Roman occupation in the vicinity. Roman buildings that have been excavated in close proximity to the quarry sites suggest this, and the apparent use of Swindon stone in Roman sites in the locality, support it. According to antiquarian John Aubrey, what became known as the Old Quarre was 'discovered' about 1640. In fact, a transaction involving this quarry was made between Richard Goddard and one Robert D'oyley in 1641. Thereafter, several small pockets of stone were opened up, notably across fields just a few hundred yards to the west of the town, and a number of lime kilns established on them, on land owned by the Goddard family, Lords of the Manor. The largest collection, south of The Sands, became known as 'the Quarries' and was worked

The Town Gardens. Even before the Swindon quarries were finally exhausted, work had started on creating the ornamental Town Gardens in 12 acres of their southern section. The Lord of the Manor was persuaded to part with the land for £700. A further £3,000 was spent on fencing off the area, landscaping and planting, and building an eccentric-style lodge for the keeper, actually over one of the tracks into the quarries. Paths were put in, borders and island beds laid out, ornamental waterways and rustic bridges constructed, bowling green, maze and tennis courts added, and a fountain and a bandstand (above) put up. The latter was an octagonal structure with an ogee-shaped roof supported by slender pillars, and a wooden dais beneath. These recreational gardens, the first to serve Old Swindon, were opened in 1894. In 1905, they were extended and a new entrance made from Quarry Road. To the right are the kiosk and aviary.

for the longest period of time. According to Aubrey, the white stone polished up satisfactorily and was in demand for interior paving in the town houses of the aristocracy.

Certainly from the mid-1600s, a number of Swindon stonecutters were working the quarries,

Jordan) and Henry Gray all carried on this trade during the second half of the 17th century, in association with roughmasons such as Thomas Little and Robert Hopkins.

Thomas Goddard appointed a steward to watch over the quarry workings, maintain his interests by reporting on new sites that had been opened so that he could impose leases, and generally ensure that they were operating within strict guidelines set out for the purpose. By the late 17th century, a number of small quarry sites had been opened up and were being worked on and around Swindon Hill. The Goddard family leased these plots to private individuals, such as Richard Farmer – mid-18th-century landlord of the Bull in Newport Street, and glover Benjamin Mills, who saw this as a potentially lucrative opportunity. In 1696, William Humphris, a Wroughton stonecutter, went into partnership with Richard Hopkins on half an acre of the quarries. Humphris continued to expand his quarry holdings into the 18th century, notably in 1707, 1726, 1732 and 1746. A 1697 list of the town's inhabitants records 11 masons including Guy, Richard and Robert Hopkins.

The lessees were responsible for fencing off their individual sections, and keeping them safe. Charges at the Court Leet show how frequently they failed to do so. The stone was exported, at first to the masons of London, but hardly in great quantities. It had to be transported overland by horse-drawn carts. However, Swindon stone destined for London was most probably carted to Lechlade and then taken along the Thames in barges. By 1700 it was in greater use locally for domestic architecture, hayrick supports, paving and gravestones. Presumably the future did not seem so bright for the industry in the mid-1700s. In 1748, the Hopkins family began to sell back their holdings, as did others such as feltmaker Henry Stichall, Moses Cattle the churchwarden, and grocer Richard Mills.

and some of the family names were still there 120 years later, by which time the traditional deposits were running out. John Williams, mentioned in a document of 1653, is the earliest stonecutter's name associated with the quarries in West Swindon Field. Thereafter, William and Richard Browne, Guy Hopkins, William Cattle (who was still there 40 years later together with Guy's son

This industry seems to have declined considerably during the last quarter of the 18th century, but it was to be revitalised by the arrival of the Wilts & Berks Canal. Then in 1790, a new seam was opened up at Kingshill, to the west of the earlier workings, and it was this that was to provide stone for the canal company's bridges. For a while, several hundred labourers found employment at the quarries. Writing in the late 19th century, William Morris, the town's first real historian, said that Swindon stone was used to construct canal-side buildings such as the little wharf house, general paving and the hump-backed bridges that crossed the waterway. It was also used on buildings in the town, by the several builders, monumental masons and sculptors who throughout the 1800s worked out of The Sands; today the western end of Bath Road. Once the canal arrived, a number of these tradespeople bought their own boats and operated their own import/export businesses, sometimes carrying small quantities of quarried stone as well as other commodities. These carriers included Swindon builder and stonemason Moses Goold, and masons William Simmonds and Richard Tarrant. In 1820, some 101 tons of Swindon stone was exported, and imports totalled almost 66 tons. Twenty-five years later, this had dropped to 44 tons leaving the town, and 24 tons coming in.

Meanwhile, the Swindon quarries continued to be worked, although by the mid-1830s, less than two-fifths of the quarried stone exported by canal 15 years earlier, was leaving Swindon. Imports of paving stone, of which the Swindon quarries once provided significant amounts, had increased dramatically. Together, this suggested that once again the quarries were in decline. There was a revival after 1840, when small quantities of stone were taken from the Swindon deposits for use in building the new railway town. (Most stone for this purpose came from west Wiltshire deposits.)

The 1855 Post Office Directory records this renaissance: 'Quarries of oolite [limestone], well adapted for building purposes, giving employment to numerous workmen, are abundant'. Yet records of the movements of stone in and out of Swindon on the Wilts & Berks Canal just two years later, show that 72 tons were exported, whilst 297 tons were brought into the town.

Even so, as the railway town developed, so the possibilities for the Swindon quarries were grasped by outside speculators as well as Swindon tradesmen. In 1846, Edward Hopkins Coale, the Swindon tailor, leased land in the quarries, and Edward Bowley of Cirencester did the same in 1851. In 1867, John Phillips, one of Swindon's principal builders, leased land and a lime kiln at the quarries, and in 1871 William Vaughan Edwards, the Wood Street ironmonger, took quarry land 'on which stands a powder magazine'. In the same year, the Goddards leased quarry plots to the Manchester architect Arthur James Seddons, Henry Farnsby Mills from Cheshire and James Stroud from Oxford. In 1877, Thomas Smith Lansdown, a Swindon architect, leased a plot. However, at no time from the mid-1800s was the yield from the Swindon quarries abundant enough, as building stone continued to be imported via the canal, for use in the town in considerable quantities.

The Quarries were accessed by a main road that bisected the workings, from The Sands in the north to the southern roadway that was eventually built up and designated Westlecott Road in 1886. The area was traversed by a network of trackways. Three short terraces of quarry workmen's cottages, ultimately 20 in number, were put up on a series of twists in the southern approach road between 1860 and 1880. Then, the whole of this section of roadway was widened, made into a right angle, and called Quarry Road. It is likely that most of the quarries were exhausted by about

1885. However, they enjoyed some popularity amongst 19th-century geologists who were much exercised when the remains of an extinct reptile named Omosaurus were reported to have been found there.

Reptiles were receiving a good press at the time, and whilst geologists argued over the findings in the quarries, down the hill in New Swindon, the canalside clay pits disclosed 'two remarkable unknown sea dragons or large reptilian whales, mounted on paddles'. They conjured up a wonderful description of prehistoric Swindon when 'it was the resort of such gigantic lizards and monstrous dragons which at that period wallowed in the rushy mire of countless ages'! A large wagonload of bones was made up under the supervision of a Professor Owen, and deposited with the British Museum.

In 1899, local builder Joseph Williams leased some grounds at the quarries and later took on nearby land to convert into a brickworks. In the early 20th century, Edwin Bradley was one of the last handful of quarriers to work the site, later buying a section outright on which the company of Edwin H. Bradley established its headquarters. Quarrying ceased altogether in Swindon in the late 1950s.

Swindon's mills and mill pond

There were two mills in Swindon at the time of the Domesday survey. One belonged to Odin the Chamberlain and the other to Odo, Bishop of Bayeux. William de Swyndon had two mills hereabouts in 1303, as did Robert Avenel and Christine his wife, in 1313. When Thomas Goddard acquired the manors of Nether and Over Swindon in 1563, they included two water mills, one almost certainly beside the pond, adjacent to Holy Rood Church on the Goddard estate. John Britton wrote about it in 1826, and William

Morris believed it to be one of the Domesday mills. It was said to have comprised a number of irregular mill buildings and outbuildings, of various storeys, some with hipped roofs. Although the whole structure was pulled down in 1856, and the mill pond drained, one can easily see where they once were. The pond was fed by a natural spring, and was divided into two sections; its lower part was enclosed, its upper section was for public use. Here the townspeople witnessed pickpockets and petty criminals being ducked, and here too carts were cleaned, and horses watered and washed. Water was carted from here for cleaning the streets, supplying breweries, stables, coach houses, water closets, baths, wash houses and for human consumption.

A windmill mentioned in a document of 1275 may have been on the same site as an 18th-century mill, built where the King's Arms Hotel stands in Wood Street. An old water mill, first documented in 1339 and variously mentioned over the next 500 years, stood 'next to the road to Wootton Bassett'. At one time owned by the Wilts & Berks Canal Company, it was demolished in the late 1880s. There was also a 17th-century water mill on the River Ray, pulled down in 1920, and its roadside mill house demolished ten years later. A corn mill existed at Okus between 1849 and 1854. Another was presumably built for the Wilts & Berks Canal Company at their Swindon wharf c.1812, but was removed c.1890.

Swindon's canal links

The idea of constructing a waterway that would link the Kennet & Avon Canal at Semington, near Trowbridge with the River Thames at Abingdon, was first raised in 1793. The Act of Parliament authorising the Wilts & Berks Canal was passed two years later. It came about in order to create a navigable waterway from the Thames & Severn

Canal bridge c.1804, Shrivenham Road. The Wilts & Berks Canal approached from the south-west where it was crossed by the turnpiked road at the foot of King's Hill that led towards Ladd's Mill and the adjacent beer house on the road to Wootton Bassett. A bridge was built at this crossing in 1803; the first to be associated with the canal in the immediate environs of Swindon. It was known as the Rushey Platt Bridge. By 1805, the canal company had all its initial bridges in place, and although these were not then named, they comprised Black Bridge, Golden Lion Bridge, Whale Bridge, Drove Road Bridge (the second to be constructed, at a crossing with another turnpiked road), Marsh Farm Bridge, Green Bridge and the bridge that carried Ermin Street at Stratton Wharf. A second wave of bridge building later in the century saw, amongst others, Cambria Bridge next to the Cambria estate in 1877, Queenstown Bridge (1885), Milton (Commercial) Road Bridge which effectively replaced Black Bridge in 1890, Whale Bridge (1893), Marlborough Street Bridge (1898) and York Road Bridge (1907). At the same time as the Whale Bridge was put in, so was the Cambria Bridge 'erected' (suggesting that the 1877 version was only a temporary affair) and the approaches on both sides were widened. Henry Joseph Hamp, then the New Swindon Local Board's Surveyor, was in charge of the work at both. The canal left the environs of Swindon to the east, beneath a little bridge that carried the track between the drovers' road and the lane to Stratton St Margaret. This is the bridge pictured, constructed of stones from the Swindon quarries.

Canal to the north, bypassing the upper Thames and part of a route that had originally been planned for the Kennet & Avon Canal. In fact, early negotiations for the Wilts & Berks were centred around protecting the interests of the latter. The Wilts & Berks' promoters envisaged carrying coal from the Somerset Coal Canal along its length, and facilitating a brisk trade in agricultural produce. The narrow boat canal reached Swindon in 1804, and it had taken three years to build the short leg from Wootton Bassett,

to the lowlands less than a mile to the south of the town. Not until 1810 was it to complete its journey to Abingdon. Together with a number of short branches, the Wilts & Berks provided just over 58 miles of waterway.

As it approached Swindon, the canal company was obliged to buy a considerable amount of land, much of which was owned by Ambrose Goddard of the Lawn; Lord of the Manor of Swindon. Goddard was a major shareholder in the company, was able to out-vote all others at the company's meetings held in the Crown (later the Goddard Arms) in Swindon's High Street, and also leased property and lent considerable sums of money to the enterprise. In practical terms, the Wilts & Berks Canal drew a line across the landscape, which must have presented a psychological barrier for the inhabitants of the old town. The five bridges they built to facilitate traffic to and from the north were also to provide for the future main thoroughfares through the new town. In this way, the canal company dictated the shape of the expansion that was to take place outside the railway village in the mid-19th century. The canal company built a run of a dozen little dwellings named Cetus Buildings, set back from the canalside towpath, on what is now the south-west side of Medgbury Road.

As the canal approached Swindon, so too did the itinerant 'navvies' who were building it. The rather respectable town on the hill was invaded by hard drinking ruffians, who were said to be generally unclean and to carry with them the prospect of all manner of communicable diseases. They doubled Swindon's population at a stroke, provided the inns with unprecedented levels of trade, and occasioned a revival of the ancient sport of bull-baiting. Previously, this barbaric sport had taken place in the Market Square, and apparently lingered until about 1810. Whilst the navvies undertook the greatest feat of civil engineering in the county to that date, others wrestled with the practical problems posed by the landscape. The marshlands south of Swindon – known locally as 'quavy gogs' – were said to be deadly, moving bogs. Geologist William Smith, engineer for the Somerset Coal Canal, spent a lot of time in the town, both as a consultant in how to overcome them, and later supervising the works. He was also retained to determine how the canal might be kept topped up at Swindon, to compensate for water seepage through the locks. Dr. Smith dug a huge well beside the canal; it struck water and filled up, before pumping equipment was brought in and emptied it! Failure here resulted in the 70-acre feeder reservoir being built at Coate, a mile and a half to the south of the town.

In 1812, the Thames & Severn Canal Company and the Wilts & Berks Canal Company proposed to link the Wilts & Berks at Swindon with the Thames & Severn at Latton, near Cricklade. The Act of Parliament authorising the North Wilts

Wharf House, also known as Fairholme. This was the fine residence of the early Superintendents of the Wilts & Berks Canal Company.

Canal was passed the following year, and the nine miles of waterway with its 12 locks was built in 1814. This link became the second largest source of imports into Swindon, conveying large quantities of what were termed 'general merchandise and sundries', salt, coal and iron from South Wales, as well as the Forest of Dean and Somerset. Stone and wheat were the main exports from Swindon via the North Wilts. In 1821, the North Wilts Canal and the Wilts & Berks Canal were the subject of a Consolidating Act that brought them both together under the Wilts & Berks Canal Navigation Company. It was this link that fell most swiftly to competition from the railways. By the late 1850s, when the Wilts & Berks to the east of the town was also suffering, and in poor condition, it was hardly in use at all as regards trade with Swindon.

The Wilts & Berks Canal had an immediate effect on Swindon's trade, although its potential was much greater than its actual success. Certainly, once it had reached the Thames, it enabled distant markets for the town's quarried stone to be more readily reached. Yet much more was imported than ever went out. Coal, coke and iron came into

Cambria Bridge is the most enduring of the bridges over the Wilts & Berks Canal, and the one that is most noticed by the general public, since it carries Cambria Bridge Road across the canal walk that links Kingshill with Swindon's central shopping area. It was erected in 1877. Cambria Bridge has long been the object of community art projects.

the town by narrow barges, and barley, wheat, wool, cheese and bacon were amongst the local exports that went through the Swindon wharf. From the very outset, Richard (banker, grocer and cheese factor) and James (draper) Strange established a business as coal and salt merchants at Canal Wharf, and within a few years had become the most important Swindon carriers on the Wilts & Berks. When James died in 1826, Thomas took his place in the firm. All the other carriers that called at Swindon originated elsewhere.

Although a directory entry for 1830 cites 'the business created by the canal' as important to Swindon's prosperity, there is little real evidence of this. Cornelius Reynolds, an insurance agent of Wood Street, was the Swindon booking agent for Richard Parker and Charles Franklin's fly boats which left the canal wharf three times a week, conveying material along its length and on to London. Other than that, there were four coal merchants operating at the wharf, and it was the potential for getting good supplies of coal along the Wilts & Berks Canal to Swindon that was to partly determine the position of the Swindon railway works. Throughout the first three decades of the 19th century, Swindon gradually built up an export trade along the Wilts & Berks Canal, mainly in agricultural products – barley, oats, corn, grain, wheat, seeds, peas, beans and cheese. Ultimately, the town was to have a number of canal wharves; New Wharf being constructed in 1857 near the junction with the North Wilts.

The nine-mile long North Wilts Canal opened in 1819, and from its junction with the Wilts & Berks Canal, it ran north along the line of part of present-day Fleming Way, then through the railway works. It left the environs of Swindon at Moredon, on its way to the Thames & Severn at Latton. There were several bridges within the town, and a number were constructed by the GWR within its works. Most notable of the former were John Street Bridge, near to the canal junction, Iffley Road Bridge, Fleet Street Bridge, Moredon Road Bridge and the famous Bullen's Bridge that was said to have been exhibited at the Great Exhibition of 1851. This picture shows the Telford Road Bridge, looking west.

In 1875, after a period in which freight transportation had gradually transferred from the canal to rail, the original company sold out to another made up of local worthies and traders. Thomas Turner, of Grove House, proprietor of a brick and tile company, was the only Swindon representative on the nine-man board. By 1895, the Wilts & Berks Canal was virtually disused through Swindon. It was so silted that only light barges could operate on it, and it had become a public nuisance. That it was not closed down at that time, was due to its value for watering cattle and drainage in the countryside, and a number of financial considerations. Meanwhile, the towpaths became public highways by right of usage, and were being maintained by the local authority.

Although the canal was dredged in 1908, it continued to be a ruin and it was eventually closed down under the Wilts & Berks Canal Abandonment Act, 1914, and partly filled in. Today, its course can be followed as a footpath right into the town centre from the west. Here it becomes Canal Walk (its 19th-century name) and part of the Brunel Shopping Centre, leading through the Parade and on through Fleming Way.

Coate reservoir

For much of its existence, Coate has been a pleasure ground and latterly a wildlife park. It was first planned in 1820 as a feeder reservoir for the Wilts & Berks Canal, to replace water that had

From the time it was constructed, until the mid-19th century, Coate Water was enjoyed by the Goddard family and the townspeople. The lake was used for boating and there were picnics, 'pleasure parties' and 'dancing parties' in the surrounding grounds. When the lake froze over, people skated on it, played football and hockey. Landlords of the local inns brought liquid refreshment, which sometimes resulted in horseplay on the ice between the sexes, and occasionally in inebriates having to be wheeled home in handcarts. On one occasion, two sheep were roasted there, and poor people received their portions by presenting single or family tickets that they had obtained at the Bell Inn in High Street. Potentially more dangerous activities included horse riding on the ice, pony and cart racing, and chasing after rabbits that were especially let loose for the sport. There are several references to the gentry of the neighbourhood and 'the old squire' (Ambrose Goddard who was Lord of the Manor until 1848) enjoying themselves there. His successor, Ambrose Lethbridge Goddard, appears not to have joined in the merriment. By the 1860s, it had all become a much more sedate affair, and the kind of place where unmarried gentlemen and their ladies stepped out, under the eyes of suitable chaperones.

been taken out by the action of the canal's locks, and so retain the required level in the canal. A number of Swindon landowners were persuaded to part with their property to accommodate the reservoir and the two-mile long feeder ditch that connected it with the canal. The 70-acre lake, opened in 1822, was formed by diverting the waters of the River Cole. It was surrounded by narrow strips of woodland that were linked to Burderop and Hodson Woods, and in consequence was from the outset, promoted as an area of considerable beauty. Fishing was positively encouraged, as anglers were told that the water abounded with fish, including pike of extraordinary size. A small boathouse was built, and a whole fleet of rowing boats, punts and even small sailing boats were offered for hire. When the lake was frozen over, people skated on it in great numbers.

Horse-drawn brakes conveyed Swindonians to Coate Water from the Market Square, and the area became known as 'Swindon's playground', although it remained outside the Borough until 1928. By 1914, when the canal had long been derelict and negotiations were in full swing for apportioning and dealing with it, the area came under Swindon Corporation's water undertaking. Its water could clean the streets, but was not for domestic use. Changing huts were put up, and for a while, swimming in the reservoir was greatly encouraged. There was a wooden diving framework, until this was replaced in 1930 by a two-stage masonry affair with a top diving board 33ft from the water. Today, Coate Water is a nature reserve and public pleasure park. This was opened by F.T. Hobbs, then mayor of Swindon, in 1935, whereupon Cicely Cousins made the inaugural dive from the new concrete diving stage into the water.

Coate Water.

Coate reservoir.

Richard Jefferies and Coate farmhouse

Close by Coate Water is the farmhouse (now a small museum owned by the Borough of Swindon, and open to the public) where John Richard Jefferies was born in 1848. Essentially a naturalist and prose poet, Jefferies remains Swindon's only man of letters. He stalked around Coate Water and the nearby Wiltshire Downs, producing some very detailed and beautifully observed work that has ensured a continuous following since it was published. In 1866 he became a journalist on the *North Wilts Herald*, which was established five years earlier in a former school building in Devizes Road. He also contributed to the *Swindon Advertiser*. A plaque marks the site of the Victoria Street lodgings he took, close to the newspaper office. Books like *Amarylis at the Fair*, *The Gamekeeper at Home*, *Wood Magic* and *Bevis* earned him a national reputation. Jefferies died at Goring-by-Sea, Sussex, in 1887.

The stone-built, 17th-century Coate farmhouse that belonged to the Jefferies family from *c*.1800. Writer and journalist John Richard Jefferies was born there in 1848. The house was extended later in the 19th century. It was bought by Swindon Corporation in 1926, part of it was opened as a museum in 1960 and the rest was let as residential accommodation. After additional rooms were opened, it became a museum to both Richard Jefferies and Alfred Williams, (1877–1930) the hammerman poet, writer and classical scholar. Jefferies was a prose poet and naturalist, much of whose works resulted from his walks around the nearby reservoir and across the downland. He began writing for the *North Wilts Herald* in 1866, lodging close by the offices of the *Evening Advertiser*, to which he also contributed, in Victoria Street. James Luckett Jefferies and John Jefferies, the writer's grandfather and great-uncle, were millers and bakers with property in High Street. The latter eventually added general grocery to his business.

Drove Road. Photographs (see previous page) of the former drovers' road show that, until well into the 20th century, this was little more than a narrow lane, flanked here and there by stone walls, but mainly lined with trees and hedgerows. It followed the eastern edge of the hill, flattened out into High Street, and then left the hilltop via Lower Town as the Coate road. Here, the road was similarly rural. After the construction of the Wilts & Berks Canal, this thoroughfare, coming from the north, crossed the bridge at Swindon Wharf. At that point was an early 19th-century residence, Canal House, by 1806 named Wharf House, then Fairholme, that the canal company built for its superintendents. It was a substantial building in extensive grounds. The first occupant was Joseph Deverall, who was there only briefly. It then passed to Canal Superintendent William Dunsford, and he was followed in 1845 by his son Henry Lyde Dunsford, who had been his assistant for a decade. They both also operated their own boats on the canal, importing coal, stone and gravel. Henry Lyde had business interests in the west Wiltshire stone quarries. During the 1860s, he carried on a heated correspondence with the New Swindon Local Board regarding the continuous flow of sewage in the canal, and demanding its removal. Fairholme was later owned by the Gilling family who farmed land on the east side of Swindon, and latterly had their English Butter Factory in Station Road. The wharf on the Wilts & Berks Canal became known as Gilling's Wharf. George Jackson Churchward, one-time chief mechanical engineer of the GWR, also lived at Fairholme which was eventually demolished in 1937. Drove Road was not built up residentially before the 1920s.

Water and sanitation

Until the mid-1800s, water was supplied to Old Swindon by the Holy Rood Church pond and a number of natural springs in the area, notably one on the road to Wroughton, and the Holy Well in Brockhill, now Drove Road. By the 1850s, most private wells had run dry, become stagnant or contaminated. Many were cesspools, and the general sanitation of the town was abysmal. Sanitary conditions in the new town were better, but declining. It was said, that in 1853, all of the old town and most of New Swindon were drawing out of contaminated wells, whilst the Great Western Railway Company was making an effort to supply filtered water to its own cottages. In this, they were thwarted by the canal company's cottages which 'soiled the water supply almost continually'. These conditions continued until proper mains began to be laid in 1866.

In 1849, a number of the town's gentry and religious leaders joined with business people, shopkeepers, traders and private individuals to present for an official Board of Health enquiry into sanitary conditions in the old town. Two years later, Superintending Inspector George T. Clark issued a damning report in which he concluded that 'the town of Swindon is particularly unhealthy'. He recommended a proper sewage system, a piped supply of water and the foundation of independent local government under the 1848 Public Health Act. The system of sewers, however, was to be two decades in the future. This report was the catalyst for the formation of the Swindon Water Company in 1857. Its prime objective was to supply sufficient water for each person in both old and new towns to have 18 gallons a day. What's more, the Company anticipated a 30 per cent population increase in the foreseeable future. Insufficient finance was raised, and at first the

Great Western Railway Company declined to co-operate. By the mid-1860s, sanitation had worsened in New Swindon and the Wilts & Berks canal was so full of sewage for the whole of its length through the town, that it was a considerable health hazard and could not be used as a source of water supply. Once it had negotiated a special contract for water to be supplied to its factories and works, the GWR agreed to help finance the venture.

The Swindon Water Company built reservoirs and waterworks at Wroughton and Okus, supplying both areas of the town. These came under the jurisdiction of Swindon Corporation in 1900, and three years later it began to develop waterworks at Ogbourne St George to meet increasing demand. As the population increased, and projections anticipated an even steeper rise, the Corporation sank its first borehole at Latton in 1931 and opened its waterworks there in 1934.

Amenities

Gas came to Old Swindon in 1841 when the Gas & Coke Company built its gas works on the west side of Brockhill, just before the steepest rise into the town. However, its service was only available to those who could afford to have the gas installed. Meanwhile, in New Swindon, the Great Western Railway Company supplied gas for street lighting throughout the railway village. In 1863, the Swindon Gas Company was formed, establishing its gas works the following year, south of Queen Street beside the Wilts & Berks Canal. This company was conscious of the need to facilitate safer journeys between the old and new towns after dark. By 1886, they were able to say that they had recently erected public lamps 'which are a great convenience to Old and New Town', adding that 'A still further benefit and convenience would be afforded by an extra lamp placed on top of the hill leading from the Old Town, from which point the light is much obscured'. Thirty years after the Swindon Gas Company established, it moved its works to Gypsy Lane.

Christ Church

Even today, one of Swindon's most outstanding landmarks is Christ Church, almost at the summit of the hill in Cricklade Street. The light on top of its spire and the building generally, are said to guide incoming aeroplanes towards RAF Lyneham. It would be nice to say that this has been an enduring symbol of the centuries; the early indication from mediaeval times of a safe haven for travellers from miles around. Not so, however. The compelling needs as the 1840s progressed, were to provide a successor to Holy Rood, and an alternative to the old churchyard which had become so crowded that deceased members of the congregation were being interred in burial grounds of other denominations. Ambrose Goddard, then Lord of the Manor, donated the site, and it was originally intended that Christ Church should be funded by levying a public rate, spread over a number of years. Plans for this were well advanced in 1848 when they were overthrown at a vestry meeting by representatives from the Great Western Railway. At that point, Revd Henry George Bailey, who was to be the first vicar at Christ Church, took on the job of organising and driving the public subscription that ultimately paid for the work.

Bailey came to Swindon in 1843, and six years later raised nearly £3,000 towards the project. Ambrose Lethbridge Goddard, MP and son of the donator of the site, gave £1,000. Christ Church was designed by Sir George Gilbert Scott in late 13th-century style. The foundation stone was laid in June 1850 and the service of consecration was held in November 1851. The church finally cost

Anderson's Almshouses, Cricklade Street. An inscription on the west wall of the building reads: 'Anderson's Hostel, A.D. 1877. From a Bequest left by the late Mr Anderson of this Town, for the benefit of the Second Poor of Swindon, the Trustees have erected this Hostel. They have also invested Five hundred pounds to provide an Annual Endowment, and One hundred pounds as a Repairing Fund for same. Henry George Baily, A.M. Vicar, John Chandler, Robert Smith Edmonds, Churchwardens, Trustees.' A Holy Rood Churchwardens' Book lists six poor women, who each year between 1765 and 1828 received a new gown under the will of a Miss Evans. Information extant on Swindon paupers in 1902, records that there were some 280 in residence at the workhouse, and just over 100 paupers in Old Swindon in receipt of 'outdoor relief' as were almost 280 at the same date in New Swindon.

£8,000 – £1,000 more than the estimate – and had 926 seats. It comprised chancel (which was redesigned in 1883 at a cost of £500), nave of three bays, north and south aisles and transepts, porch and western tower with a broach spire. The clock and bells were transferred from Holy Rood. The Goddard family continued to embellish the church, adding a marble and alabaster reredos, new altar and altar steps in 1892, an alabaster font in 1905 and a pulpit the following year. In 1927, they paid for a window that was designed by Martin Travers which went into the north transept in memory of Fitzroy Pleydell Goddard. This incorporates a view of the Lawn, the family coat of arms and those of Christ Church, Oxford where he attended the university. A side chapel, designed by Harold Brakspear, was added in 1935. The original wrought iron, 6ft tall, octagonal font cover that had been stored for

Christ Church, Cricklade Street. Revd H.G. Baily went for the sympathy vote when soliciting subscriptions for a new church in 1849. The result of an overcrowded churchyard at Holy Rood meant that 'sadly harrowing and revolting to the feeling are... scenes too sad and humiliating for repetition here, deeply painful to every churchman'. His circular letter quoted the parents of a young man who had to be buried in a Dissenting burial ground, who said: 'The pastor to whom he looked in life for guidance, in death he was compelled to forsake'. The Lord of the Manor gave £1,000, Revd Baily contributed £50 and amongst the other worthies of the day who put their hands in their pockets were Henry Lyde Dunsford, Superintendent of the Wilts & Berks Canal (£20), solicitors James Bradford and William Morse Crowdy (£50 each) and leather dresser and currier Robert Reynolds (£20).

about a quarter of a century, was beautifully restored by Bernard Oxborrow in 2001.

Revd Bailey was fundamental to the movement which set up the Old Swindon Local Board and the New Swindon Local Board in 1864. He also built King William Street School which was completed in 1871, and became rector at the nearby village of Lydiard Tregoze in 1885. He is buried in the churchyard at Christ Church. Along the southern side of the churchyard is a run of dwellings that originally comprised four almshouses, Anderson's Hostel. This low, two-storey building, with decorative bargeboarded gables, triple lancet mullioned windows and iron casements, was designed in Gothic style by Swindon architect William H. Read. Thomas Barrett built it in 1877 on the site of some very old thatched cottages. Funding came from a bequest by Alexander Anderson who died in 1874. In 1993, they were converted internally into self-contained flats for the elderly, winning the Thamesdown Borough Council's Conservation & Design Award.

Town Hall and Corn Exchange

The idea of building a permanent market house was first floated in 1848, and four years later the Swindon Market Company was formed to put it into practice. The new market house was also to provide accommodation for the County Court, Petty sessions and other public business. The building was designed by Sampson Sage, a local architect, and built by George Major of Horsefair, now Devizes Road. In reality, it was little more than a sack office and store room, and in 1853 its lower part was leased to wine merchant William Brown. His business became Brown & Nephew in 1862 and Brown & Plummer 20 years later. A small, square, two-storey building abutting the east side of the Town Hall became the latter

Corn Exchange, Market Square. In its early days, the Corn Exchange was the venue for lectures and readings; the Old Swindon equivalent of the 'improving' readings that took place at the Mechanics Institution in the new town. The latter appear to have been reasonably successful, particularly those given by the writer George Grossmith. The *Swindon Advertiser* sometimes complained that the readings in the Corn Exchange were boring, went on too long and were hardly relieved by the indifferent piano playing between the pieces. The readers were often berated, either for not properly familiarising themselves with the pieces, or for failing to get into the spirit as intended by the writers. They should, the paper announced on one occasion, 'confine themselves to pieces that are within the range of their own comprehension'. The tower was a landmark in the old town from the moment it was put up. George Deacon made the clock with 4ft-wide illuminated dials. It struck the hours on a 2cwt bells and the quarters on two smaller bells.

company's cash wine stores, and they used the tunnels beneath the Market Square for storage. The cellars are said to be haunted by the ghost of Stephen Lawrence, one-time company cellar man, who drowned himself in the church pond. The hall above the wine stores was leased to the County Court and used by the Swindon Bench of Magistrates for the next 20 years. The public room, which could accommodate 600 people, was used for all manner of public meetings, those of various organisations, and balls. By common consent it became known as the 'Town Hall', but by the 1880s was being advertised as the 'Assembly Room'. In 1891, all public affairs were transferred to the newly-built Town Hall in Regent Circus, New Swindon.

For some years, the town's businessmen had been calling for a corn exchange when, in 1865,

Town Hall, Market Square. The Town Hall may not have been an administrative success, and it is certainly true that when the Corn Exchange was added, local opinion regretted that a better position had not been found for what was widely regarded as a most handsome structure. It is difficult to visualise the two as other than a single building, and it is this integrated backdrop that has since characterised the old town Market Square. It was here that tethered bulls were once baited by dogs (later 19th-century maps still referred to it as the site of a Bull Ring), and early in the 20th century, people of the old town boarded trams that took them down the hill. Here too, hunts met, political gatherings took place, and modern-style fairs were held with stalls and roundabouts.

Ambrose Goddard, Lord of the Manor, finally agreed to let the site of two old cottages behind the Town Hall. Forty-three architects submitted plans for a corn exchange. Wilson & Wilcox of Bath won the commission with a Grecian-style building that had an 80ft tower to the east. Swindon builder John Phillips got the contract. During building, he fell from the roof to the cellar, sustaining serious injury but escaping with his life. Over the door are the words 'Blessed be the Lord who daily loadeth us with benefits'. A door was put in between the Corn Exchange and the Town Hall, so that in the event of a substantial ball or some entertainment that might command a large audience, the rooms in the latter might be used as supper rooms. An entrance was also built from the poultry market, so that the directors of the entertainments, and those who participated in them, would have separate access to that of the ticket holders. There was a continuous series of windows that opened into a triangular market house with a fountain at the centre, and the whole area was surmounted by a glass dome. The entrance was beneath the tower, through a spacious, tiled vestibule.

The exchange was opened on 9 April, 1866, one week before formal business began. Directors, shareholders, local tradesmen and others

Parliamentary elections, 1886. This crowd is gathered at the front of the Town Hall in the Market Place of the old town, awaiting the declaration of the 1886 poll. This was the parliamentary election in which M.H. Nevil Story-Maskelyne (Liberal) defeated Sir John Bennett and B.C.F. Costello. Prior to 1918, Swindon was in the Cricklade constituency which, before multiple-member constituencies were abolished by the Act of 1884, returned two members. The Great Western Railway's Sir Daniel Gooch survived several elections, and was joined in Parliament by Ambrose Goddard in 1874. Story-Maskelyne first took his seat in 1880, and was returned three further times in succession. When Swindon ... e a constituency, its first MP, Sir Frederick W. Young, was a Conservative. The town turned Labour for the first time in 1929 with ... on. Sir Charles Addison; Banks got it back in 1931, but Addison swung the 1934 by-election. He lost by just 75 votes the following ... nd Swindon remained Conservative until the end of the war. Then followed ... a quarter of a century of Labour domination in the town.

assembled at the Goddard Arms and, fronted by a brass band from New Swindon, proceeded in dignified procession to the exchange. Inside, 400 people sat down to dine, although ladies were segregated into the gallery where they were afterwards given cakes. John Toomer, the coal, salt, corn and seed merchant, was in charge of the musical arrangements. He engaged the singing duo Hamilton & Dawson, and Harry Sydney, a well-known comic singer of the day. The champagne, provided free of charge by Brown & Nephew, had an inevitable effect. There were numerous toasts, and as the proceedings dragged on, the noise got louder and the participants ever more jovial. After repeated, unsuccessful calls for order by the Chair, a toast was drunk to 'the ladies'. Solicitor James Bradford got to his feet to reply on their behalf whereupon the band, who had only been booked until six o'clock, struck up the national anthem and left the room.

Those members of the organising committee who were sat close by, and heard the odd note or two above the general din, came to the same conclusion, and also left the building. A new chairman was elected on the spot so that the revels could continue. Harry Sydney's contribution to the opening ceremony is not known, but at the inaugural ball a few days later, he sang an 'impromptu' and extremely embarrassing song relating to the Corn Exchange, called *In a quiet sort of way*. However, this was clearly a society affair, with the guests dancing to a Hanoverian band supplied by Milsom & Son of Bath. Four innkeepers clubbed together to provide a cold buffet – William Westmacott of the Goddard Arms, William Godwin of the Bell, John Godwin of the King's Arms and John Washbourne of the Mason's Arms. The guest list included just about every well-to-do tradesperson and holder of public office from Old and New Swindon, and Daniel Gooch and A.L. Goddard. It was an

occasion of great splendour in the best Victorian tradition of the times, with numerous toasts and indulgent, verbose speeches.

The cellars below the Corn Exchange were at once leased to Brown & Nephew as additional wine stores. Together with the cellars of the adjacent Town Hall and the tunnels, they then had well over an acre of storage space. Office accommodation was leased to the same firm (by then Brown & Plummer) in 1887. When the company of wine merchants put up its name plate on the side door of the Town Hall in 1911, it was charged one penny per annum!

By 1880, the large hall in the Corn Exchange was furnished and licensed for stage plays; dressing rooms had been provided and the auditorium could seat 1,000 people. The hall was used as a roller skating rink for several years before the outbreak of World War One in 1914. It was leased to Clifford Cunningham as a cinema in 1919 and remained so, being named the 'Rink Cinema' for 30 years. Thereafter, it was refurbished, redecorated and used as a general dance and social hall called the Locarno Dance Hall, and later as a venue for wrestling promotions and pop concerts, and latterly a bingo hall.

Swindon's newspapers

Swindon's first newspaper, the *Swindon Advertiser*, was founded by William Morris (d.1891) as a four-page tabloid monthly in 1854, and printed on a hand press in Victoria Street. Morris was at one and the same time reformer, liberal and moralist. Wiltshire's first 'penny paper' became a weekly the following year when stamp duty on newspapers was repealed. In 1861, it began to be printed by steam power, using a boiler and engine built in the Swindon works of the Great Western Railway. By that time it had a circulation of 5,000 copies. The paper was

Victoria Road, newspaper offices. The façades of William Morris's mid-19th-century, purpose-built office block and printing works are one of the architectural statements of Old Swindon. Nos.99 and 100 Victoria Road are each of three bays, and both have moulded eaves with a fine table of brackets, and first floor Venetian windows. The ground floor in each case is of rusticated ashlar and the print works façade has quoins. Swindon's first newspaper had a page size of 15 inches by 12 inches, had just four pages, and was printed by hand on stiff paper.

renamed *Swindon Advertiser* and *Wiltshire, Berkshire and Gloucestershire Chronicle* in 1870 and has been published daily since 1898. It has been titled the *Evening Advertiser* since 1926.

Also in 1861, the *North Wilts Herald* was established in Devizes Road by a group of businessmen, and transferred to Bath Road after Joshua Henry Piper became the proprietor in 1865. A daily from 1882, it remained in the Piper family until 1922 when it was acquired by the then owners of the *Evening Advertiser*.

William Morris (1826–1891). The son of a bookseller and the father of a builder, William Morris was the epitome of the portly, bearded Victorian. An outspoken liberal and moralist, he used his position as editor of the town's first newspaper to forcefully promote his views. This made him an incredibly influential figure in the town, although there were occasional legal actions against him and he was once banned from reviewing theatrical productions at the Mechanics Institution for regularly criticising them. William was born at Wotton-under-Edge, Gloucestershire, and came to Swindon at the age of four. For many years, his father had a bookseller and stationer's shop at 13 Wood Street, before the premises were taken over by Deacon the jeweller. William became a man of property, who was once in confrontation with the Swindon Water Company for refusing to pay water rates on nine of his houses in the old town unless they gave him a bulk discount! He was also Swindon's first real historian, although he wrote much contemporary history spanning his own life, and relied heavily on hearsay and personal reminiscences. Many of his pieces first appeared in the *Swindon Advertiser* and were gathered together for publication in his wonderfully rambling 1885 book *Swindon Fifty Years Ago*. William Morris died in the Wilberforce Temperance Hotel, Bournemouth.

In 1942, this paper became the *North Wilts Herald and Advertiser*; the *Wiltshire Herald and Advertiser* in 1950, and its present style of *Wiltshire Gazette and Herald* in 1956.

During the late 1870s, the short-lived *New Swindon Express* was published from a number of addresses in Bridge Street, in the new town. At the same time, a simultaneous edition of the Devizes weekly newspaper, the *Wiltshire Times* was being published in Bridge Street, and from Isaac Hunt of Regent Street one could obtain the *Bath Herald & North Wilts Guardian*. The Victoria Street printer Robert Astill was simultaneously publishing the *Wilts & Gloucestershire Standard* with the Cirencester edition. Swindon remained a two-newspaper town – the *Evening Advertiser* providing the daily news, and the *Wiltshire Gazette & Herald* acting as a digest of the week's events with a bias towards the rural community – until 1962. This was the year in which politician Woodrow Wyatt's Banbury Press published the town's first litho-printed, colour newspaper, the weekly *Swindon Echo*, which lasted four years.

Medical matters

Swindon had no general hospital before the Victoria Hospital was opened in Okus Road in 1888. Of course, there had long been the pest house, an ancient foundation, well to the west of the town on Okus Field, and in the early 1870s, the Great Western Fund Medical Society had erected a hospital specifically for accident victims in its New Swindon works. The hospital for infectious diseases at Okus eventually came under the joint auspices of the town's two Local Boards. In the 19th century, people seeking admittance had firstly to present themselves to the Inspector of Nuisances, who lived in the centre of the old town! The hospital for infectious diseases was demolished and superseded by a red brick

When it opened for business, the Victoria Hospital was a modest affair. The hospital for infectious diseases at Okus had been closed and dismantled. The New Swindon Local Board had rented a property in Wroughton and had graciously agreed to admit patients from the Old Swindon Local Board area. It meant that the only hospital on the hill was the newly opened Victoria, on a site given by A.L. Goddard, which is why his wife laid the foundation stone on Golden Jubilee Day, 1887. The hospital had five beds in the male ward, five beds and two cots for children in the female ward, and two beds for the use of accident victims. Persons presenting for admission had first to be assessed by a committee and then examined by the resident doctor. Patients could be visited on Tuesdays, Thursdays and Saturdays between three and four o'clock in the afternoon. And anyone disposed to a guided tour of the building, could be taken around on Wednesdays between two o'clock and four.

isolation hospital built to H.J. Hamp's design, in Gorse Hill in 1892, and extended nine years later. It had wards to deal with diphtheria, typhoid and scarlet fever, the latter being perceived as the most prevalent. It is now the Hawthorn Centre.

The Swindon and North Wilts Victoria Hospital, built to W.H. Read's design in Okus Road in 1888, was an altogether more grand affair that befitted a sizeable town. It cost £1,960 to build and furnish, and was voluntarily funded. The original design catered for another wing, and this was added six years later at a cost of £700. Further extensions took place in 1923 and again in 1930. The foundation stone for the latter extension was laid by the Countess of Radnor, and the opening ceremony was performed by the Marchioness of Lansdowne. Here was an institution which could boast recognition by the General Nursing Council as a complete training

Kingshill House, Bath Road. This substantial and flamboyant villa was built in the 1840s. The entrance is beneath a three-stage tower with moulded string courses, constructed to look like a Georgian church tower. It originally had a pierced parapet with acorn knop finials. The doorway beneath opens into a spacious stair hall. During the 1870s, Kingshill House was occupied by Richard Bowly, the brewer, wine and spirit merchant whose premises were at 10-12 High Street. At some time, it was a doctor's residence, and it became the maternity hospital in 1931.

school for nurses. The mid-19th-century Kingshill House, almost opposite the Victoria Hospital, was opened as a maternity hospital in 1931 and subsequently became a mental health unit. Princess Margaret Hospital was built at Okus 1957–60.

Expanding residential Old Town

In 1801, the population of the hilltop town was 1,198. In 1891, the last census before Old

Swindon and New Swindon became administratively a single authority, Old Swindon's population had increased to just 5,543. Its industrial neighbour, which in 1841 still had fewer people than the old town, nonetheless leapt to nearly 33,000 within the next half century. Yet whilst the new town's developers were obsessed with building on every piece of land that became available, Old Swindon's expansion was much more gentle. One of the earliest photographs extant, is of a crowd scene at the northern end of Victoria Street, immediately before it became a descending trackway through gardens and orchards. Its point of entry into the old town was

Victorian Terrace. Before the 1840s, Victoria Street appears to have been home to neither persons nor trade of any note. Then we read of tradespeople establishing there; amongst others, tailor Charles Cannon, William Coates the boot and shoe maker, baker William George, drapers John Tarrant and Robert Woolliams, and carpenter Thomas Walters. We can imagine them taking the opportunity to support the professional people living in the grand, three-storey houses that had just been put up further along the road. The architects of Old Swindon from the mid-19th century were much influenced by a pseudo Italian Romanesque style, and they found that the more prosperous of the town's tradespeople and professional gentlemen were prepared to indulge them. The little paired windows, thick string courses, moulded and flowing cornices, had not before been attempted in this town of flat façades and plain, blind parapets. Some of the later houses in Devizes Road are of this style, but they are best seen in Victoria Street, now the old town end of Victoria Road. After they went up, there were changes. Jane and Ann Smith had their ladies' school here; Joseph S. Smith, high bailiff of the County Court, took up residence; printer, bookseller and stationer Abbott Dore gave added credibility to the street, as did the prosperous William Vaughan Edwards.

High Street, Sewell's Bakery. By the 1870s, both High Street and Wood Street had, to a considerable degree, shed their cottage industry traders. High Street then comprised substantial business premises, with a mix that reflected its proximity to the old markets, and a more recently acquired status for commerce and gentry. Thomas Deacon and Daniel Smith, saddlers and harness makers, were the most obvious links with the past, and Deacon & Liddiard's Vale of the White Horse Repository opposite the Market Square, commanded the largest business ground area. Deacon & Liddiard were also auctioneers and had a cattle sale yard further towards Devizes Road. Almost next door to them were the auctioneers Dore, Smith & Radway. Doubtless the suppliers of leather to the harness makers also called on boot and shoe maker John William White at No.36. Traditionally, this was a butchers' quarter and there were still four of them trading from separate premises; Thomas & William Chapman, John Bond, James Biddis (later taken over by Eliza Biddis) and Edward Smith. James Upton carried on his trade of fishmonger at No.1, and across the road at No.2 was Joseph Walter the ironmonger. There were three grocers, wine and provision merchants; Philip Hawe Mason & Co., James Hartland, and White & Akerman. Matilda Monk the confectioner was at No.38. William John Smith's chemist shop was at No.18, and there were three drapers; Eli Heath, James Blake Daniel and Albert Horder. Tailor and outfitter George Pakeman was at No.22, and William Povey was at No.15. John Humphries the hairdresser was at No.3, next door to the Goddard Arms. Next door to the Bell Hotel resided two surgeons, John Blount Fry and F.E. Streeten. Brewer and wine merchant Richard Bowly lived at No.10. Solicitor Henry Kinneir lived at Redville, a substantial house beside the drive to the Goddard's manor house, and his business of Kinneir & (Henry Coggan) Tombs was also in High Street. Their colleague, J.E.G. Bradford, was on the opposite side of the road – the offices of Bradford & (William) Foote – with a garden that was flanked on either side by a brewery.

illuminated at night by a single stanchion gas lamp. It shows a street lined with a terrace of three-storey houses in vaguely Italianate style. Today, their façades remain substantially unaltered above street level, where they have long succumbed to shop frontages.

In the 1850s, these houses were home to the families of some of the town's more prosperous businessmen, and the genteel and finely clothed participants in the picture are clearly of this order. When they acquired the properties, they must have thought their positions to be unassailable; adjacent to what was effectively a green belt with fine views to the north, and in a position where they neither saw nor heard the less savoury elements of the old town. In about 1849, William

Morris moved into the street where, five years later, he was to publish the first issue of the *Swindon Advertiser*. At the time, he styled himself bookseller and stationer (which had been his father's occupation) and letterpress printer. His premises, where the newspaper's offices continue today, and where once lived Charles Haines, the watch and clock maker, were just a stone's throw from those of Abbott Dore. He was proprietor of a circulating library, was once the town's only printer, and was father of auctioneer and appraiser William Dore. In fact, this company had come about mainly in order to print posters and catalogues for the latter. It remained in the family until 1877 when it passed to Robert Astill.

Situated on the corner of Victoria Street and Bath Road, Astill's home and printing works were a landmark property in 19th-century Old Swindon. (His works offices were in a separate building next door in Victoria Street.) We have a good description of the premises, put together when they came up for sale in 1903, and were said to be suitable for any 'large business or offices'. There was an entrance lobby from each thoroughfare, leading to drawing room, reception and breakfast room, kitchen, scullery, coal house and greenhouse. The drawing room and reception room were at the time occupied by W.H. Bush, the hairdresser. Astill himself had a stationery and fancy goods business in the breakfast room. The dining room was on the first floor, together with three bedrooms, and dressing rooms, and there

Albert Street corner, *c.*1880. Albert Street never became fashionable and remained a backwater in the town. However, the last thatched cottages lingered here until they were pulled down in the 1960s. When this picture was taken, only three named traders are recorded: Daniel White had a shop at No.26, Martha Scapelhorn had a bakery, and Joseph Gosling was selling beer.

Albert Street, Old Swindon. This narrow lane, at the centre of Old Swindon's 19th-century 'red light' district, existed long before it was named, following Queen Victoria's marriage in 1841. It was the haunt of the lowest labourers and had several beer houses, one of which became the Rising Sun. It also had the Rhinoceros, where it was said that almost any vice might be witnessed or indulged in. By the 1840s, however, some of the tenants in this collection of little thatched cottages had aspirations of trade and respectability. John Wheeler set up a bakery, William Hayward established a carpentry business, and William and Reuben Horsell undertook plastering. Laurence Lawrence had a brief career as a purveyor of 'quack' medicines. The greatest change came about when a number of females established themselves making clothes and bonnets in Little London; Martha and Emma Butler, Sarah Mulcock, Mrs Ann Hayward, Mrs Sarah Rudman and Mrs Ann Keylock all set up in the trade and thrived. Meanwhile, Lucy Rogers' beer house and that of William Waller helped to lower the tone of the area, and doubtless Joseph Pagett's shooting saloon did little to improve it. In 1857, a fracas occurred that resulted in Mrs Rogers fleeing the Rhinoceros pub, in her nightdress, accompanied by her daughter and pursued by Mr Pagett. He knocked her to the ground, whereupon she struck her head and died. He was subsequently charged with her manslaughter.

were four large bedrooms and a linen closet on the second floor. There were three cellars, of which one was given over to wine. Outside, gained by a carriage entrance from Victoria Street, there was a coach house with bedrooms for servants above it, outbuildings, gardens, and a stable and yard that were let on a weekly basis to a Mr Greenaway. These premises epitomised the way of life for a prosperous Swindon trader and householder in Victorian times. Here was a substantial building that had been reorganised internally to facilitate a number of retail activities, the owner carried on a trade that was not his primary one, and parts of the premises at street level were sub-let to others. Yet around these multi-business premises were also the trappings of aspirational home life; several bedrooms to accommodate a large family, servants to look after them, and a well stocked wine cellar in the basement. These were the kind of people who were having new villas built for them in Bath Road from the 1840s.

Also living in Victoria Street were William Vaughan Edwards, principal in the Wood Street

King's Arms, Wood Street When the busiest frontage in Swindon was put up in the later 1860s, with its flamboyantly presented coat of arms, it must have seemed that a new architectural era had dawned in the old town. Hereabouts there stood a windmill, associated with which John Godwin Snr. had a dwelling and bakehouse, probably with a frontage on to Wood Street. Godwin seems to have established an alehouse on his premises *c*.1840, since before that date he figures only as a baker. The King's Arms is first mentioned in 1842, with Godwin as innkeeper. In 1864, John Godwin Jnr. leased land behind the inn, possibly the old windmill site, from the Lord of the Manor and clearly set about rebuilding the existing premises and extending them. Son of a baker, nephew of the owner of the Belmont Brewery and clearly an entrepreneur in his own right, Godwin Jnr. capitalised on his associations, added the coat of arms to his literature and designated the King's Arms an 'Agricultural and Commercial Inn'. His is the neo-Gothic, three-storey façade of five bays in brick with stone window dressings and quoins. The compact arrangement of double lights separated by shafts and capitals, the little gables with their roundels, the recessed porch given prominence by the fussy, flanking bay windows and the soaring, corbelled out chimney stack, make this an uncompromisingly exciting building.

ironmongery firm of Edwards & Thompson, and the coach builder Richard Mason. William Dore also lived there, as did John Tanner and Robert Woolliams who were tailors. Whilst Victoria Street was considered suitable for two ladies' schools in the early 1850s, John Longhurst's nearby common boarding house, and a couple of beer sellers, might have given cause for some concern.

Prospect Place continued to be built up over two decades, and the road become very fashionable. It had fine views of the countryside, and by the 1850s, several people of independent means were living there. By the 1860s, the way between the railway village and the old town was still a difficult route amidst fields. It began at the northern end of Prospect, descended the hill to Eastcott and the farm buildings close by present day Regent Circus, and thence to the Golden Lion bridge over the Wilts & Berks Canal. A number of the more affluent tradespeople that moved out of Victoria Street settled in Prospect Place. Here, in the mid-1800s, could be found builders George and Charles Major, William Affleck the agricultural engineer, accountant William Hartley, Sampson Sage the architect, surgeon Charles Axford and the private residence of William Warner, one-time superintendent of the police force. These were all people of influence in the district, giving credence to Prospect Place as an aspirational thoroughfare.

Yet even as the early photograph was taken in Victoria Street, it is likely that its fate as the main linking thoroughfare had been settled. For early in the 1850s, orchards were sold that had previously prevented any progress of the street to the north. These were bought for residential development, at about the same time as land became available to the east, bordered by Cricklade Street and its continuation into the old drovers' road. This led to the development of Belle Vue Road in the mid-1850s. Here was the old town reasserting itself

Prospect Lane old police station.

Prospect Lane police station. A fascinating series of postcards were produced during the Edwardian period, on the subject of burglaries in Swindon. One shows a policeman (his uniform looks more like that of a station porter) looking at a newspaper headline that reads 'more burglaries in Swindon'. His comment is: 'Why can't the people do as I ask 'em, stay home at nights and give the Police a chance!!' The second shows a police inspector with a magnificent walrus moustache, speaking with a very fashionably dressed lady outside the police station. Fair householder: 'Oh! Inspector. Someone has broken into my house and stolen... Inspector (raising his hand to silence her): 'My dear lady, impossible! you must be mistaken!! there are no burglars in Swindon!!!' The third in the series shows four policemen seated around a table in the police station, gazing at a crystal ball. The superintendent asks, 'Well Sergeant can you see anything?' and the sergeant replies, 'Yes! I can see two men but I can't tell who they are!' The Wiltshire County police force was established in 1839 and soon afterwards, William Warner was installed at Prospect Place in Swindon as the Superintendent of Police and Inspector of Weights and Measures. He was succeeded at Prospect Place by Superintendent Henry Haynes.

with a range of middle-class properties and more fashionable villas, curving away from the narrow, mean row of limewashed and thatched cottages that were Little London, Albert Street and Back Lane. It was to be nearly 40 years before Belle Vue Road actually went anywhere, so in 1865, Union Row was developed, linking its southern end with

Police houses, Eastcott Road.

Victoria Street. People walking this route had to pass the notoriously disorderly Rhinoceros public house at the end of Albert Street, and another corner beer house within a few footsteps. A few years later, a second beer house was established opposite the Rhinoceros, with an adjacent brewery. It must have seemed that Albert Street was pushing back the fashionable tide of Belle Vue Road. This is not to say that aspiration and opportunity were entirely missing from the Little London area.

From the moment the Great Western Railway works established in New Swindon, there was also a perceptible shift in the style of Old Town trade. Existing companies, particularly those in Wood Street and High Street, increased the areas of their shop premises and their ranges of stock, and began to advertise themselves in much more expansive ways. Some of these advertisements actually solicited the patronage of New Swindon residents, suggesting that there was no comparable establishment to be had in the area. Other traders, particularly in the commercial sector, began to add on products and services. One of the most noticeable effects that the nearby population explosion had on the traditionally labouring families of the old town, was to encourage their entrepreneurial spirit. By 1860, there had been a proliferation of sole traders, working out of cottages in the poorer parts of the town, such as Newport Street, Albert Street and Back Lane. A case in point is Elijah Rushen, who in the mid-19th century, was variously described as living in Little London, Cricklade Street or even High Street. We meet him as a furniture broker in the 1840s, and can trace his career as a carrier, a beer retailer, and a second-hand clothes dealer. Elijah, and people like him, simply saw opportunities in the need for increased trading capacity, and took them! This led to what was described in the late 1870s as 'a remarkable development of business

premises in the last decade' with 'scarcely a place of business that has not been rebuilt, enlarged or improved'.

A period of development in the decade following the insertion of North Street at the end of the 1860s, saw a whole warren of streets colonising the north-west slopes of the hill between Victoria Street and Eastcott. In the mid-1870s, Victoria Street pushed a little more to the north, building up itself and developing King John Street and Stanley Street at right angles. The 1880s and early 1890s saw developers working around the quarries and the town gardens, south of Bath Road and The Sands. First Lethbridge Road was laid out in the mid-1880s as a western continuation of Newport Street. Large, detached houses continued to be put up alongside Bath Road, and less grand homes lined Devizes Road. On land between them, fashionable, middle-class terraces appeared. By the end of the century, Goddard Avenue was partly built up, to the west of the main quarry site, soon to be followed by the Mall.

Okus was a sandy, grassy, uninhabited area beloved of children. By the end of the 19th century there were still but few buildings south or west of the Victoria Hospital. Thereafter, the road petered out roughly where it was joined by the track that led to Okus Farm and the fine 17th-century thatched barn that was demolished in 1975. West of this were the Okus quarries and associated gravel pits, a terrace of four houses for quarry workers, allotments, and another track to the little group of Okus Cottages. Just before the track that linked all of this terminated at the hamlet of Okus, it skirted the Swindon Water Board's reservoir. It was not until the 1930s that the land between Okus Road and Kingshill began to be built on. With the exception of the Mall, a stylish Edwardian thoroughfare, and Belmont Crescent off the very old, but uninhabited Mill Lane, little residential development took place on the quarry side before the 1940s. Then Portland Avenue went in adjacent to the quarry at Okus Cottages, and in the 1950s Tithe Barn Crescent ran around the reservoir site towards the old Okus barn which was then still standing.

The late 19th-century businessmen of the old town continued to consider themselves rather superior to the new trade in New Swindon. A group of them demonstrated this in 1884 by forming an archetypal gentlemen's club, the Swindon Town Club, at Fairview in Bath Road. The original shareholders included Frederick John Brown and Alfred Plummer, partners in the firm of wine merchants. There was auctioneer James Radway who was famed for his cart-horse shows and sales at Deacon & Liddiard's Vale of the White Horse and Carriage Repository. Thomas Hooper Deacon, who established that firm in 1871, was also a shareholder. His premises, which fronted High Street almost opposite the Market Square, were very important to Swindon in the later part of the 1900s, and it was largely due to the Repository that the trade in horses flourished. So important was it, that architect William Read, the Old Swindon surveyor, was commissioned to design the stabling for over 100 horses. It also featured a large paddock at the rear with some 300 yards of 'gallop'.

Shareholders in the Swindon Town Club also included founding solicitor John Coplestone Townsend, whose firm of Townsends has for so long occupied the old house at 42 Cricklade Street. Local butcher Edward Keylock had a stake in the enterprise, as did Thomas Turner who owned the Drove Road brickworks, engineer James Shopland and a bank manager, Sydney George Stock. Not unsurprisingly, a founding member was Joshua Henry Piper who clearly thought that here was a pulse of Swindon's luminaries of commerce and trade, on which the proprietor of the North Wilts Herald should have his finger. The club included a reading room, billiard room and card room. The venture appears never to have been hugely profitable, but it continued faithful to its original founders' vision for more than a century. The Swindon Town Club closed its doors for the last time in the early 1990s.

Local government

Before the local boards were set up, Swindon was governed by the vestry; people who were elected from qualifying residents of means. They were mostly responsible for the work of the parish officers, financial matters affecting the fabric and day-to-day running of the church, and the relief of the poor. Henry Noad of a long-established Swindon family, baker and parish clerk, is an example of one who held office for several decades from the end of the 18th century. Although Old Swindon petitioned in 1849 for powers to set up a local board under the Public Health Act 1848, this was not adopted and the town remained a parish for the next 15 years. In 1864, following the possibility that Swindon might be included in a sanitary and highway district with nearby Highworth, the Local Government Act 1858 was applied to both sections of the town. The New Swindon Local Board held its first meeting on 27 April, 1864 at the Mechanics Institution, under the chairmanship of the GWR's William Frederick Gooch. The Old Swindon Local Board met for the first time on the following 10th August, at the Town Hall, Old Swindon, in a room rented from The Swindon Market Company. Their chairman was the grocer Philip Hawe Mason. Even at this level, it demonstrated the cultural distinction between the established settlement on the hill and the industrial newcomer. The Local Boards remained for 30 years when, in 1894, they both became Urban District Councils.

Regent Circus. It was in the early 1880s that the idea came about of building a square adjacent to York Place; a residential terrace that came to form the north side of present day Regent Circus, initially suggested as Trafalgar Square. At the time, there was open countryside south of Regent Street, east of Eastcott Hill, and north of the houses that had been erected in Dixon Street. It was soon clear that the square had the potential to attract a number of fine villas. Although these were put up on the east and west sides, this was not to be a leafy residential area. Shop frontages went into York Place, the Town Hall was erected in 1891, the Head Post Office was built on the corner with Princes Street in 1900, and horse troughs were put in on each side. This became very much a confluence of traffic between the old and new towns, and early photographs of Regent Circus show it going in all directions. A clockwise one-way system was adopted there in 1932. This was followed in 1934 by one-way traffic around the nearby island at the foot of Victoria Road. (The County Ground/Shrivenham Road intersection where the town's infamous Magic Roundabout is now, had its first roundabout installed in 1936.) See also next page.

Regent Circus, early 1930s.

By 1890, the New Swindon Local Board had plans to build their new public offices adjacent to York Place, then the name given to a terrace of houses adjacent to the Rifleman's Arms. This was both psychologically and strategically an excellent position for the new town to establish a landmark building, being halfway between the railway village and the town on the hill. The architect was Brightwen Binyon of Ipswich, who placed a 90ft-high clock tower above the rather grand west front, and built his piece of neo-17th-century Dutch architecture all in brick, with stone dressings and balcony, gables, finials and cupolas. Internally, there was – and is to this day – a spacious hall with pillars and arches, and a magnificent sweeping staircase rising to a suite of offices. When the building opened in 1891, these were occupied by the Board's senior officials and those of the county court, whilst other rooms were available for public meetings.

The prospect of a single Swindon was a burning issue for at least the last two decades of the 19th century. It was said that the population approved the idea and influential commentators such as the *Swindon Advertiser's* William Morris were heavily in favour. However, even latterly, both councils were suspicious of each other's motives and wary of the status of their respective districts in a united Swindon. The NSUDC was more powerful in every way, had the backing of the town's overwhelming industry, and was therefore the prime instigator of moves towards amalgamation. The separate UDC arrangement lasted until 1900 when the two combined and Swindon Borough Council came into being under a Charter of Incorporation. It was the last borough status to be granted during Queen Victoria's reign. The Regent Circus offices of the New Swindon UDC became the council offices of the new Borough, and remained so until 1938 when the Civic Offices were opened in Euclid

Town Hall, Regent Circus. Here was the New Swindon Local Board making a statement in 1891, with a building that dominated the Swindon skyline, in a position where it was also clearly visible from the old town. At the time, Regent Street had progressed eastwards as far as York Place, with Regent Place behind it, and just around the corner, Eastcott Terrace was built in what was to become Princes Street. Only recently had a small square been laid out. On the eastern side there were a number of large villas, the Methodist central hall, retail premises and Holy Rood Roman Catholic Chapel. The Town Hall was built of pink brick with stone banding and dressings, with horizontal and vertical string courses. It presented a riot of windows, pediments, pierced parapets, finials, cupolas and turrets. The main entrance porch faced Regent Street, and had a veranda. All of the other doorways were also fairly grand, suggesting that the local authority personnel who entered them, all held offices of some importance. From the moment it was built, the New Swindon Town Hall became a focal point for large, outdoor meetings and places where visiting worthies were displayed to the people. The Town Hall clock has been known to chime eccentrically over the years, once in the 1960s striking 24 times at three o'clock in the afternoon! Eventually, local government outgrew the building and it was all removed to the Civic Offices, built for the purpose, in 1938.

Street. The ground floor of the Regent Circus building now houses Swindon's reference library, whilst the rooms above are occupied by a multi-media arts venue and dance studios.

In 1889, at a meeting of the New Swindon Local Board, James Hinton suggested that at the end of 20 years, the population of Swindon would be sufficient for the town to 'become a county'. In 1913, the Council did investigate the possibility of acquiring County Borough status. Under the Local Government Act 1888, no application could be considered from any authority with a population of below 50,000. The 1911 census for Swindon showed that this was exceeded by just 751.

Under the local government reform of 1974, Swindon was included with surrounding villages in the Borough of Thamesdown. The name was an absurd and universally unpopular combination of 'River Thames' and 'Wiltshire Downs'. This was reversed, to virtually unopposed acclaim, when Swindon became a unitary authority in 1997, and was designated the Borough of Swindon. In 1993, the Borough Council and the Swindon Chamber of Commerce put together a joint public relations venture, Swindon – City for the 21st Century – aimed at raising awareness of the town as a precursor to possible city status. Although the partnership mounted an exhibition in London, the whole project lost impetus. In 1999, the Borough Council made a formal, but unsuccessful, bid for city status. Another unsuccessful bid was made for 2002.

North of the hill *c*.1800

At the start of the 19th century and throughout its first few decades, habitation around the hill consisted of a handful of fairly isolated

Golden Lion, Regent Street. The Golden Lion Public House was built late in the 1840s, close to a farm track where it crossed the Wilts & Berks Canal at Eastcott. John Cross ran it in 1848. The stone lion itself sat above the parapet over the entrance to the pub, although it was latterly taken down and re-erected beside the front door. A wooden swing bridge, about 12ft wide, was put up here across the canal in 1806, and the road on either side was made up by public subscription in 1845. For many years, there was no lighting in this area, although it was a major thoroughfare, said to be in almost constant use, day and night. In 1864, followers of the Free Christian Church raised enough money to put a lamp by the Golden Lion. This was such an improvement that it became the catalyst for lighting, by public subscription, other streets in New Swindon that were not directly owned by the GWR. By the mid-1860s, public lamps were erected along Westcott Place as far as the turnpike, along Bridge Street and to the top of Eastcott Hill. The swing bridge was replaced in 1870 by an ornate, iron lift bridge made in the GWR works, and a footpath was added by public subscription seven years later. The bridge featured a hump-back walkway, huge hollow stanchions and ball finials. The bridge was operated by a complicated system of weights and pulleys, and a mechanism below ground level. It was demolished by military personnel, in 1918. The Golden Lion pub continued until the mid-1950s. The original lion is said to have met its end in some local authority yard, but a replica, by sculptor Carleton Attwood, was put up close to the former site in 1977.

farmsteads, single cottages or little groups of dwellings, and the occasional small manor house. These were connected by a few trackways or lanes, several of which formed the basis of thoroughfares that exist today. There were a number of hamlets and manors whose names we still recognise. Coate, Broome and West Leaze lay around the southern perimeter, Walcott was to the north-east, Russia (Rushey) Platt, Westcott and Even Swindon were joined directly to the north with Rodbourne Cheney in the far distance. Immediately to the east were Westlecot and King's Hill. In the centre of it all was the hamlet of Eastcott, then little more than a couple of dozen cottages and houses south-west of present-day Regent Circus. The lane down the hillside threaded through them towards a couple of farms.

At a point where the old drovers' road that skirted to the east of Eastcott veered off towards the Marsh, the Wilts & Berks Canal Company erected an imposing villa for its manager, next to Swindon Wharf. To the west of this lay the canal company's infamously unsanitary cottages at Cetus Buildings, then there was Upper Eastcott Farm. This bordered orchards, and was close to a handful of houses where Regent Circus now stands. A lane ran north from here, then circled towards Lower Eastcott Farm. People who passed this way could call at a cottage beerhouse known as the Red Cow, whose name survived in that of its nearby public house successor. That too, fell foul of road-widening and rebuilding when Princes Street was remodelled in the 1960s. However, in the early 1800s, this was the area that was destined to become the commercial centre of New Swindon.

Another track ran north-east towards the farm access bridge (later to become the Golden Lion Bridge) that was placed across the canal in 1806. A track that skirted Upper Eastcott Farm met the latter roughly where the Rifleman's Hotel now stands in Regent Street. Yet another lane ran down the west side of the hill, through the hamlet of Eastcott. These latter two converged on the canal, almost connecting with an ancient trackway that ultimately led from the lane, towards Wootton Bassett along the north side of the canal. This was certainly known as 'le flet' by the 16th century; it was to become Fleetway and to be incorporated into Westcott Place and Fleet Street. Another lane wandered north towards the hamlet of Rodbourne Cheney. There were isolated cottages, sometimes groups of two or three together, amidst the lanes and tracks, and occasionally dotted about here and there in fields. This is how the land of the great retail and commercial centre of Swindon presented in the early years of the 19th century.

The railway village

The Great Western Railway Company's 7ft-wide, broad gauge line reached Swindon in 1840, five years after Parliament approved the construction of a railway between London and Bristol. From the outset there was considerable difficulty in providing accommodation for the employees at the Swindon railway works. The solution was to build a model village, originally planned in 1841 as 300 cottages. The design is traditionally ascribed to Sir Matthew Digby Wyatt, although there is no hard evidence that it was other than Brunel's own. Building was carried out on land north of the Wilts & Berks canal that the Company had bought from John Henry Harding Sheppard, at the expense of Joseph D. Rigby & Charles Rigby, the builders. Bath stone was used, most probably from the cutting out of Box tunnel, and stone from the Swindon quarries. The contra deal was that Rigbys should recoup their outlay by leasing the cottages to the Company, and through profits from the station refreshment rooms. In the

GWR model village. The planned village was remarkable for its symmetry, which it kept as it extended, and passed on in essence to those speculative builders who developed mini-estates around it. As early as the 1840s, a hierarchical structure had appeared on the ground in the emerging village. The rows of small, stone cottages were receiving their larger 'end stop' houses, facing the public thoroughfares. The works manager's house, placed away from those of the workers, but nonetheless where they would encounter it just before the entrance to the works, gave inspiration and encouragement. The GWR's Bristol Street school kept the children away from the village, but within the shadow of the church, from which they gained spiritual guidance. And far enough removed to the east, to psychologically separate work from play, was the cricket field that later became the park. The deeds of the school stated: 'And it is hereby further declared that it shall be a fundamental regulation and practice of the said school that the Bible be daily read therein by the children and that no child shall be required to learn any catechism or other religious formulary or to attend any Sunday school or place of worship to which respectively his or her parents or guardian shall on religious grounds object that the selection of such Sunday school and place of worship shall in all cases be left to the free choice of such parent or guardian without the child's thereby incurring any loss of the benefits and privileges of the school'.

GWR village street. The railway village was planned very much in accordance with Victorian hierarchical values, and feelings for comparative social status. It was also in order to engender a sense of community, and a bit of publicity on the part of the company. Overall, the best aspects faced the railway line, so that travellers passing through would get the impression that here really was a superior development. However, the whole estate was based on the main entrance to the works, originally set off by a grassed area. This presumably had a calming influence, in strong contrast to the conditions 'inside'. The better houses for company foremen and the like, were on the ends of the rows, to give the tenants a greater feeling of space. Professionals in the works enjoyed properties which faced away from the rows of workers' cottages, such as on to High Street and Park Lane, where their occupants could largely ignore the everyday life in the village. The buildings were put up in High Street for traders, some of whom were already well known in the town. Others quickly achieved the kind of status in the community commensurate with these bigger premises. It was in this area too, that the public buildings – the market, Mechanics Institution and hospital – came to be built. Their position reminded men daily of the various ways in which the GWR company sought to help them improve their lot, and provided for them when they were in difficulties. Finally, the multi-gabled station managers' houses – dark, brooding and imposing in their own grounds, underlined status in the most obvious way.

event, work on the village began in the early 1840s. Some 243 dwellings were built by 1853 and it was to be the mid-1860s before the estate was completed. By 1851, Swindon had a population of 2,371. Four years later, this was officially estimated at over 2,500.

The terraces were built in straight rows, back-to-back. A central, paved alleyway at the rear was approached through archways at each end. This gave back access to the brick-walled yards with their wash houses and privies. Many of the smaller cottages were 'one-up-one-down' with a

tiny front garden and pairs of front doors almost touching in a kind of v-shaped porch. By this device, and the impressive façades, the casual observer might not have realised that here were actually the smallest of double tenements. Larger cottages had twice the accommodation, and larger houses still, some with gables, were built at the ends of the rows. These tended to be occupied by foremen at the works.

The parallel streets in the railway village, four on each side of the square, were each named after

GWR village backs. In the 1850s, here was one of the most insanitary areas in the two towns. Livestock were kept in the houses, backyards were awash with the contents of overflowing cesspits, and the drains leached substances into the kitchens. The occupants' answer to all of this was to scoop up the undesirable effluent in buckets and throw it into the streets, where it immediately contaminated further areas of the village; worryingly where children played. In 1853, several children died here as the result of an outbreak of typhus fever. Many lectures were given at the Mechanics Institution, elsewhere in New Swindon and also in Old Swindon, based on this outbreak, the dangers of other deadly diseases, and matters of sanitation in general. Illnesses such as typhoid and scarlet fever were regularly reported on and debated in the local press of the day, and there were frequently very pointed references to the less than acceptable conditions to be found in the railway village.

a town with a GWR station. The initial terraces of Bristol Street, Bath Street (renamed Bathampton Street in 1901), Exeter Street and Taunton Street on the western side, were put up 1842–3. The eastern ranges of London Street, Oxford Street, Reading Street and Faringdon Street, were built between 1845 and 1847. The axis road of this estate linked directly with the railway company's main thoroughfare into the works, and for a while, the square between the two blocks of terraces was grassed and railed off. Larger buildings adjacent to the square, partly intended as shops, went up 1845–7. The more imposing houses, occupied by the Company's management, were put up in Church Place at the far west of the village, during the first half of the 1850s, as was the little run of houses that faced Faringdon Road. The management's houses overlooked the park and

were close to St Mark's Church. There was severe overcrowding in many of the company's houses that accommodated both families and lodgers.

For aesthetic architecture and a sense of history, the railway village is as good as it gets anywhere in Swindon. All that has disappeared from the original plan, and that at the hands of the railway company, were two large executive villas that stood north of London Street and the company's school building at the western end of Bristol Street. Even after the company had built its magnificent school building in College Street, boys continued to attend the original Bristol Street school. The boys of the railway village were often a problem to the company, and famously, in 1859, Daniel Gooch issued a warning notice. 'It having come to my knowledge that many of the boys of New Swindon are very unruly and mischievous in

Baker's Arms, Emlyn Square. Built on the corner of Bath Street and High Street in the mid-1840s, it was, by 1846, leased to land surveyor William Perris. However, this was a beer house and baker's shop, and it seems likely that the business was connected with Richard Philpott Perris – flour factor and baker. The baking was carried out at the rear of the shop. In 1848, the lease was taken over by Richard Allnatt who was styled baker and beer retailer, and who was to remain in occupancy for 30 years. Allnatt removed the bakery to premises in Taunton Street off Church Place. There, he had two bakehouses and two ovens, and made deliveries by means of a horse and cart which he kept beside a yard at the rear of the premises.

their conduct, especially during the evening when property is frequently damaged and (as on a recent occasion) life endangered, I hereby give notice that any person in the service of the company reported to me as being disorderly, firing cannons, or making an improper use of firearms in the Village be discharged, and as the parents in most cases are to blame for not checking such bad conduct amongst their children, I consider it my

duty for the protection of the inhabitants and the Company's property to hold the workmen in the factory responsible for the behaviour of their children, and shall not hesitate to discharge any man who allows any of his family to commit such offences.'

At the centre of the railway village is the new town's former market place, originally called High Street, and named Emlyn Square since 1900. The

Glue Pot, Emlyn Square. This was not originally intended as a public house, although internally it is identical to the Baker's Arms on the opposite side of the square. The Glue Pot has the nicest façade of the former commercial buildings hereabouts, with its gables and little round, blind windows in each. It was built as a three-storey house and shop on the corner of Oxford Street and Reading Street during the 1840s, and appears to have been in the occupancy of a Mr Fidler; trade unknown. An early lease of 1848 ascribed it to David Dunbar, a sculptor of Pimlico, and in 1850 it appears to have been William Warner's wool and linen drapery. The shop occupied what is now the public bar, with access to parlour, kitchen and scullery at the rear. The retail area was converted to a public house c.1850, and the downstairs was added to and remodelled in the 1860s. At one time, this pub was called the London Stout Tavern.

plan for High Street was that it should include a number of shops, and it was not long before James Copeland established his butcher's business there. Mason's put in a branch of their grocery and tea establishment in competition with Edmund Webb; Richard Perris had a bakery, James Trego the chemist and druggist was in residence, William Warner opened a linen drapery, James Praed set up as a hairdresser and Edward Frankis opened the Railway Dining and Coffee Rooms. Knapp's family grocery was taken over by William Fisher, who added stationery to the business.

Church Place. The inhabitants of what was originally called Park Road, this most westerly run of houses in the GWR village, had the best view of the pleasure gardens. They also had a grandstand seat for the annual juvenile fete which, since it involved tens of thousands of people, they must have viewed with some apprehension. Park Road was by far the most logical name, but it was changed partly to avoid confusion with Park Lane on the opposite side of the park, and partly because of its proximity to St Mark's Church.

A number of public houses were associated with the village. By 1841, the Queen's Arms was open east of the station (it became the White House after 1910). At the station itself there was the Queen's Hotel Refreshment Rooms and Posting Establishment, and opposite there stood the Queen's Tap from 1843. The Wholesome Barrel was built c.1841 close by the Crown Eating House. Both were adjacent to the North Wilts Canal, roughly where it was crossed by the railway line. The Cricketers on the former High Street was planned as a licensed house and opened in 1847, just preceding the Baker's Arms near Bristol Street, and the Glue Pot of 1850, which at one time was called the London Stout Tavern. Much of the railway village was bought by Swindon Borough Council in 1966, and the following year was statutorily listed as being of special architectural or historical interest. The Council's award-winning modernisation and improvement scheme for Brunel's 'model village', took place between 1969 and 1980. The end-of-terrace railway foreman's house of c.1842 in

Faringdon Road has been refurbished to its likeness in the last quarter of the 19th century, and is open to the public.

The Mechanics Institution

The Mechanics Institution was the GWR's employees' serious attempt to better themselves, and the Institution was formed as a society within the railway works in 1843. The Institution's first president was Daniel Gooch (1816–1889), who was the GWR's Locomotive Superintendent until 1864, the year before he became chairman of the company and was elected as Conservative MP for the Cricklade Division of Wiltshire. Gooch did not live in Swindon, although he appears to have been a go-between, balancing the, at best, ambivalent attitude of the company towards the workforce, with the aspirations of the people themselves, as expressed through the work of the Institution.

At the Institution building, concerts, social events and lectures began to take place. Whether

The Mechanics Institution, officially 32 High Street, always had a good press. It was said that 'it had the effect of diverting the minds of the younger portion of the inhabitants into a channel pregnant with good things and throwing a genial influence around the neighbourhood'. By the time the foundation stone of the Institution was laid in 1854, the Institution (the body that had been formed in the railway works for the betterment of its employees) was taking up considerable space on the GWR premises for its various activities. For some time after the New Swindon Improvement Company was formed, the GWR schoolroom was used as the Mechanics Institution's concert and lecture hall, and a large room in the factory became the reading room and library. The schoolroom soon became too small for the size of the musical entertainments, the numbers of people wishing to attend them, and the increasing programme of lectures. The GWR allowed the Institution to transfer its events to an unused workshop in the factory, but this was difficult to access. At the same time, the library and reading room soon outgrew its space. From the very beginning, the Institution building was proposed to serve all residents (not only Institution members) of New Swindon. It comprised, on the ground floor, housekeeper's room, offices and cold water bathrooms, a 1,250 sq.ft. reading room, 170 sq.ft. library, a 408 sq.ft. coffee room, and 612 sq.ft. dining room. On the top floor there was to be a 3,040 sq.ft. hall for concerts, lectures, public meetings, entertainments, etc. with a 1,250 sq.ft. theatre stage. The library of the Mechanics Institution closed in 1961 and its stock was sold. Some documents went to the County Records Office in Trowbridge, Swindon Public Library service acquired material relating to the railways and other items of local history, and the rest was bought by the general public. The building was first sold to a private developer in 1986, since when it has fallen into disrepair.

comic productions or sacred music, philosophical debate or popular discussion, the Institution was determined to educate, amuse, and raise both the standards and the morale of every type of artisan or clerical worker who cared to join. Ten years later, the New Swindon Improvement Company was established specifically to erect public buildings, improve and extend New Swindon. Underlying this were the problems posed by insufficient traders for the increasing population in the new town, as well as a lack of necessary services and social infrastructure. The new Swindonians had to trek across fields and navigate the steep footpath to the old town, in order to obtain more than the basic provisions. The Improvement Company was to remain an influential force for betterment in the town until 1899.

Its Mechanics Institution building, designed by Edward Roberts, was opened in High Street, New Swindon in 1855 and enlarged 50 years later. Crucial to 19th-century betterment were the reference library, the reading room with its stock of newspapers and journals, and a large dance hall. This room was also used as a meeting place for various societies, public lectures and occasional amateur dramatic productions. After a devastating fire in 1930, the reading room area was remodelled and opened the following year as the 700-seat Playhouse Theatre. For a while, weekly productions were held there, but it never achieved its full potential as a theatre.

From the very beginning, the Institution bought reference books, popular and academic non-fiction, and classic and contemporary works of fiction. They were all made available to residents of the town as well as people living outside. There was a chess and draughts room and, in the hall, all manner of musical recitals, dramatic productions, lectures and recreational classes took place. The building also housed the town's first public baths. At the same time, the young men of Old Town had a similar venue in Victoria Street where they could read newspapers, magazines and books, or play chess or draughts in the rooms of the Church of England Young Men's Association.

By 1879, plans had been developed to occupy the site of the adjacent market house with a new Institution building to the design of Brightwen Binyon. This would have a spacious lecture hall, and a general theatre, whilst the existing hall was to be converted into a reading room, next to an enlarged library and committee rooms. The building was extended in 1893.

Great Western Railway: the beginnings

There is the myth that the position of the railway works came about when I. K. Brunel and Daniel Gooch were inspecting the marshy ground, with its rabbit warrens, in the vale to the north of Swindon. In one version, Brunel threw a stone, in another he wasted a sandwich. But the result was his stated intention to build his works at that spot. One of the problems with this apocryphal tale is that it has been put forward for both the building of the locomotive works in the early 1840s, and the building of the carriage and wagon works a quarter of a century later!

Brunel famously travelled in a personal brougham, the enclosed four-wheeled carriage with an open driver's seat on the front, in which he was conveyed whilst laying the entire Great Western line. The brougham contained a small bed, seating accommodation, desk space and crimson leather cushions. Brunel used it as office, dining room and bedroom wherever he went. For many years after the line was built, this vehicle was kept in the works at Swindon, and shown to visitors (who from very early on were welcomed after 3.00pm on Wednesdays) as part of a small museum of the company's history. The museum also included Stephenson's *North Star* locomotive, built in 1835 and put on the Great Western Railway instead of going to its original destination in Russia.

In 1841, the GWR's directors ratified Brunel's decision about the workshops. Swindon station opened in 1842 and the Great Western Railway's works became operational in 1843. The works were established here mainly because this was the point at which it was expedient to change engines to cope with a steeper gradient to the west of the town. It was also intended to be the junction of the Cheltenham & Great Western Union Railway's Cheltenham line with the GWR main line, and that would need a reasonable station. Also, the proximity to the Wilts & Berks Canal's Swindon wharf, with its links to the West Country canal network, promised a good supply of coke and Somerset coal at reasonable prices. The GWR Company even thought it might be able to draw water from the canal and the reservoir at Coate. Water for the works was initially taken, by agreement in 1843, from the North Wilts Canal.

Swindon station

The most enduring fact about Swindon station is that, for 53 years from the moment it opened in 1842, every train stopped there for ten minutes. It meant that the engines could be changed and all passengers could take advantage of the luxuriously appointed, first class and second class refreshment rooms. It was important to mid-Victorian Swindonians to know that their queen and members of her family had been entertained there. The station comprised a building of three floors on each side of the main lines, linked by a covered walkway. The two Georgian-style station blocks were identical in shape and external elevation, first floor plan, and in having cellars, kitchens and

Great Western Hotel, Station Road. The 'Queen' was a popular dedication for Victorian station hotels. Swindon had three, yet none of them aspired to the kind of 19th-century grandeur as achieved by, for example, the Queen's Station Hotel at Chester. The Swindon versions were built as drinking houses with stables attached, but with limited accommodation. In 1870, the Great Western Hotel opened in opposition to the other Queens. Architecturally, it had moved on considerably from the hotels of the 1840s, but it was not until it was extended and remodelled in 1905 that it presented any kind of serious approximation to the levels of accommodation achieved by station hotels elsewhere in the country.

station workers' accommodation in the basement. The ground floor was mostly taken up by the two refreshment rooms, separated by rows of columns. The two upper floors accommodated the station hotel, with bedrooms on the north side and lounge areas to the south. J.D. & C. Rigby who had the refreshment rooms on lease, sub-let to

Queen's Arms, Corporation Street. Almost a speculative venture, for when this hostelry was built in the 1840s, it could hardly have been more isolated. Perhaps this is why, in the 1860s, the auctioneer William Dore was able to hold livestock sales here. Interestingly, these were so successful that six years later, the GWR company axed plans to build their own cattle sale yard on company land near the Queen's Arms, because Dore had a monopoly there that they considered to be unassailable.

Queen's Tap, Station Road. Imagine this little building standing in isolation opposite the station in 1841. It is not much changed, except that the stables are no more and it is dwarfed by multi-storey office blocks, including that above the station. In the 19th century, cattle and horse sales were held in the yard at the rear.

Samuel Young Griffith, owner of the Queen's Hotel at Cheltenham, and the whole complex became known as the Queen's Royal Hotel and Refreshment Rooms. Neither under his occupancy, nor that of later incumbents, were the food and drink up to the expected standard, and the enforced stop became something of a mixed blessing for travellers. John Rouse Phillips bought the lease in 1848, and the Company eventually bought back the rights in 1895. The original station was demolished in 1972 and a modern station and office block was built on the same site.

The railway works

When the Great Western Railway's locomotive works started up on their doorstep, it must have seemed to the occupants of agricultural Swindon that an awesome industrial monster had been unleashed on the marshlands below them. Nonetheless, agricultural labourers came down the hill to try their hand at the rather more remunerative jobs the GWR had to offer. The works were established and developed along the north side of the railway line. Ultimately, the works were to cover more than 320 acres. The workforce approached through a long tunnel that led from the High Street square, underneath the line, past the time office and administration block. This very same tunnel is now a walkway, linking the shopping centre of modern-day Swindon with the retail outlet village that has been created out of the railway workshops. The first building to be commissioned was the locomotive repair shed, which began operations in 1841 using contract labour. Machinery was installed the following year. No doubt many Old Swindonians took advantage of conducted tours of the works on Wednesday afternoons, and probably came back time and again as the premises were extended over many years.

GWR Works tunnel, London Street. The main entrance into the works, and the main point of exit when the hooter indicated the end of a shift, was the tunnel north of the Mechanics Institution, that led under the lines. Now it is a ten-minute walkway to the retail Designer Outlet Village that was opened in 1997, the STEAM railway museum, the gallery and shop of the National Monuments Record, and a number of other conservation projects. It was said that the sound of men running through the tunnel, which was kept open 24 hours a day to facilitate changing shifts, was reminiscent of a stampede of animals. It was down this tunnel too, that retired workers and their families went to the little office where they could order their entitlement of wood and coal. Several generations of the same family followed each other 'inside'. In 1924, King George V and Queen Mary visited the works, when 76 men, who had each served the railway company for a minimum of 50 years, were brought together for their inspection, dressed in their best suits and flat caps.

Once engine building began in 1846, the works claimed to be turning out the best and most powerful engines in the world, and on show was exactly how it was done. Visitors would have heard that this was no local industry. Here was the centre of broad gauge engineering, even though the works had built its first narrow gauge locomotive in 1855. A narrow gauge engine shed and large narrow gauge carriage storage shed were built at Swindon in 1872. At the time of the conversion to narrow gauge (4ft 8½") in 1892, the company's complement of rolling stock was brought to Swindon, where it was either converted or destroyed. Here too, was the point of manufacture for all the permanent way rails. It took the Swindon works less than two weeks in 1846 to build *Premier*, its first broad gauge passenger locomotive. Five years later, when turning out on average one engine per week, they constructed the *Lord of the Isles*, in its day the fastest broad-gauge locomotive.

The locomotive division was always by far the biggest and most visually spectacular part of the works, employing the greater proportion of the company's workforce. It included the rail mills – later renamed the rolling mills. Here the rail mills' furnaces were 'seething iron incessantly belching forth huge lumps of white metal for conversion into rails for the company's permanent way'. The carriage and wagon works were added in 1868 when the company took the decision to centralise all operations on Swindon. This meant that they had to provide not only the facilities to carry out the core building work, but also to manufacture everything necessary to achieve this. The company even developed its own brickworks at Rodbourne to make the bricks that went into many of its

GWR workshops. The GWR was almost entirely a male domain until around the mid-1880s. It was then that the company began to take pity on families whose breadwinner had been killed or severely injured whilst carrying out their occupation in the works, and found suitable jobs for some of the widows or wives involved. There were many things they could do, particularly in regard to fabric coverings and trimmings for the carriages. Certainly by this time there had been an inordinate number of reported fatalities and lost limbs amongst the GWR employees at Swindon, and it all seemed to be regarded more as unavoidable occupational hazards than anything that reflected badly on the company. Women were first taken on as clerks in the railway works in 1912, opening up new opportunities for a section of the community that had hitherto been employed almost exclusively as domestic servants, in nursing and the tailoring trade, or as shop assistants.

Carriage Works, London Street. The carriage works, designed by T.G. Clayton, were built 1869-72. Today, much of this is divided into industrial business units. Internally, the building retains its original cast iron pillars and vaulted brickwork. The original carriage and wagon works comprised around two dozen shops. The men built the wooden frames and constructed the carriages around them, and carried out carriage repairs. Here was a sawmill; there were fitters of many types, carpenters and cabinet makers, painters, fabric makers, plumbers, metal smiths, trimmers and upholsterers, and general mechanics. There was also a disinfecting plant. The carriage and wagon department was extended in the late 1950s to accommodate the requirements of the diesel era.

works' buildings. At one level, for example, the machine shop was making the component metal parts for assembly into a locomotive. At another, from 1872, the ladies of the sewing shop, who shared their area with the French polishers, were making carriage trimmings. This was seen as an important step in that it 'gave occupation to the unemployed wives and daughters of the mechanics and others in the town and neighbourhood of Swindon'. In accordance with Victorian sensibilities, they were provided with a separate entrance 'remote from the works in which the sterner sex are engaged'.

Each division of the works consisted of a number of 'shops', all distinguished by a prefix letter (in the case of the locomotive works) or number. The quantity of 'shops' increased as did the diversity of activities undertaken at the railway works. A taste of what was taking place in the locomotive division alone, may be gleaned from this list:

'A' Erecting, machine and wheel shop, 'B and C' engine repairers in what came to be known as 'the hospital', 'D' carpenters, turners and fitters of carriage and wagon wheels, 'E' electricians, 'F' general smithy, 'G' formerly boilermakers, then millwrights, 'H' carpenters and pattern makers, 'J' iron foundry and chair foundry, 'K' coppersmiths and sheet metal workers, 'L' painters, 'M' electricity plant, 'N' carriage wheel fitters, 'O' paint shops, later tool room, 'P' boiler making, 'Q' angle iron manufacture, 'R' general machinery and fitting, 'S' wheelwrights, later springsmiths, 'T' brass workers and gas fitters, 'U' brass foundry, 'V' tender making, 'W' turners and machinists, 'X' permanent way component makers.

The boiler and tender-making shops were opened in 1875, and the parts made in them were for the company's locomotives and the marine engines used by their fleet of ships. There is a lovely, typically Victorian-style description of the locomotive repair shop: ' a 'hospital' is provided for maimed and disabled 'patients' requiring admission within its walls; such being the skill and potency of the treatment here administered that perfect convalescence is always secured'. Associated with the stamping shop – colloquially the 'hot shop' – was the company employee (Owen) Alfred Williams (1877–1930). Known as the 'hammerman poet', Williams was a self-taught scholar and linguist who spent his meal breaks behind the great furnaces learning Latin and Greek. His most enduring book *Life In A Railway*

Designer Outlet Village, GWR Works. Ironically, it took American foresight to recognise the potential value of the Grade II-listed, 19th-century GWR workshops to Swindon's regeneration and economic growth. The whole retail mall, which opened in 1997, has been created out of the industrial buildings that the GWR developed over a long period of time. The earliest building included is the original wagon paint shop of 1846, and the latest is probably the pattern makers' shop of 1924. Other workshops that have been converted include the coppersmiths' shop, and those of the toolmakers, brass finishers, brass foundry, blacksmiths, machinists, boilermakers and tank makers. It took unprecedented co-operation between developers, national and local organisations and businesses to convert these into Europe's biggest covered retail outlet centre, and to market it as a major tourist attraction. Where locomotives and engine parts were once made, some are now displayed, together with some of the 19th-century, overhead lifting cranes that moved it all about.

GWR foreman's house, Faringdon Road. The dimensions of the railway village, the narrow alleyways and the little back yards, are all as they would have been when originally laid out. When No.1 Faringdon Street was built, c.1861, it was a three-up-three-down, end-of-terrace house of note. Since 1980 it has been a 'living museum', and the town council's guidebook charts its continued occupancy for 118 years. For the first 40 of them, it was the family home to two generations of railway workers. Refurbished, it lives in a time warp around 1900.

Factory described his own experiences, and he wrote a number of other books about the countryside.

From the late 1860s, the company's whole works were protected by a Shand Mason steam fire engine that could be made operational in about seven minutes and was capable of discharging over 300 gallons of water per minute. It was backed up by two dozen strategically placed fire extinguishers and as many water hydrants. The fire engine, and accompanying brigade of men, were also loaned out when required in New Swindon and the surrounding district.

As the works expanded, entrances were made in Station Road and Rodbourne Road. Initially the company summoned its workforce by tolling a bell. In 1867, the New Swindon Local Board licensed a steam hooter that could be heard up to ten miles radius of the works. This hooter was described as being 'a boon to all the country round' in that it 'performs a useful moral work' and 'by its voice thousands are warned of the approaching hours of labour; men are imbued with habits of regularity, and regularity begets order in the general affairs of life'. These sentiments cut no ice with Henry, Lord Bolingbroke, whose annual sojourns at his Lydiard Park country house were disturbed by its sound,

The GWR's three-storey, seven-bay pattern store was the place where draughtsmen worked on the patterns, the forms were made and the moulds were filled. The two upper floors held the blueprints and the moulds that were used in the castings and repair work. Although the big design tables have gone, many of the original racks remain. The workshops were at ground floor level, and the pattern makers' canteen was in the basement. Each one of the ceilings was barrel-vaulted in brick, and the floors were composed of black wooden blocks the size of small bricks. The whole building was constructed around steel pillars and girders, with wide, semi-circular, iron doors leading to exceptionally wide staircases between the floors. An ornate, circular staircase led from the upper floor into a metal turret on the roof, giving access to huge water tanks that once supplied the GWR village. Heavy machinery was hauled up the outside of the building, by means of a pulley system, on to the appropriate floor. Items were let down internally by similar means, through a series of trap doors in the barrel-vaulted ceilings. In front of the building is the locomotive turntable that features in many historic photographs, for it was here that new engines were brought to be pictured for GWR publicity. Two floors of the pattern store were renovated and converted into a public house, the Pattern Store Bar, which opened in 1998. Because the turntable is still in working order, the pub's business manager has the job of turning it once a week in order to ensure that the bearings are running free. There are a number of blocked-up tunnels beneath the pattern store building, some of which are 40ft underground, that appear to lead towards the locomotive works.

The former GWR weigh house is now the home of Archer's Brewery that was founded in Swindon in 1979. The original building was put up in red and black brick in 1906, and a breeze block section indicates where it was extended some years later. It was here that the locomotives were brought, by means of a single track, to be weighed and balanced. The interior was refurbished in the late 1920s, and contemporary pictures in the brewery show that the balancing machines then used were all named and dated 'Henry Pooley & Sons Ltd, Birmingham & London, 1930'. For most of its working life, the weigh house was surrounded by railway sidings.

apparently to the detriment of his heart condition, at a time when he was at home nursing an injured leg. Bolingbroke argued that there was no point in having something that sounded over so great a distance, when it was clearly impossible for any worker who heard it from that far away to get to work on time anyway. In 1873, despite unanimous opposition from the populace, he succeeded in a legal action to revoke the hooter's licence to blow. It was, however, only a temporary injunction. A new atmospheric hooter was installed in a different location, thus continuing both to meet the original judgement and rouse the workforce.

One of these, before he was dismissed from the company's employment in the 19th century, was the gaunt George French (1841–1906). It was said that in his younger days George had been 'champion walker of Wiltshire'. He was nicknamed 'Hooty' after his ability to mimic the hooter's sound using small pipes, and was also known as 'Hooty-up-a-gas-pipe' because he appeared to sleep in the empty pipes on the railway company's land. French survived by making paper windmills and using them to barter with children for saleable commodities. He was a well known figure around New Swindon, usually accompanied by a square, covered wooden barrow in which he kept his belongings.

A most important, and well-liked GWR official was Joseph Armstrong (1811–1877), who in 1864 became Superintendent of the company's whole Locomotive and Carriage Works at Swindon. Born at Newburn, Northumberland, he knew many of the railway pioneers such as Hawthorn Edward Woods, and assisted in the early journeys of Stephenson's *Rocket*. In honour of the former, Armstrong gave the name *Hawthorn* to the first broad gauge locomotive to be designed and made at Swindon after he took charge of the works. An influential Wesleyan, he was said to be retiring, diffident and as conscious of doing right by the workforce as he was of his obligations to the GWR. Armstrong was variously chairman of the New Swindon Local Board, president of the Mechanics Institution and a director of the Swindon Water Company. Today, he is remembered in Armstrong Street near the station, Newburn Crescent to the west of the works on the former site of his residence Newburn House (demolished 1937), and his memorial in St Mark's churchyard. The other railway luminary was George Jackson Churchward (1857–1933) who was also the superintendent, as well as the GWR's chief mechanical engineer for 19 years from 1902. A brilliant engineer, his great successes were the 4-6-0 Star series, City and County locomotives. He too lived in Newburn House, and was one-time chairman of the Local Board's successor, the New Swindon Urban District Council. When the Borough of Swindon was created in 1900, he became the first mayor. Churchward died as a result of being hit by a train whilst crossing the line in fog. He is commemorated in Churchward Avenue at Rodbourne.

The Swindon railway works initially employed just over 400 men; it had 2,000 men in 1851 and at its height, over half a century later, this had risen to nearly 16,000 people and accounted for three-quarters of the town's working population. They famously built the GWR's King Class locomotives, *King George V*, being visited during production in 1924 by the King and Queen Mary. During the 1930s, employment was considerably

Water Tower, Bristol Street. This cast-iron landmark was constructed in 1871 to supply water to all parts of the Great Western workshops. It is 64ft high and built in three storeys, each of three bays. The 50,000 gallon tank sits on a platform at the top. The tower is very close to what remains of the GWR school building.

reduced at the railway works, and although sons continued to follow their fathers and grandfathers 'inside', fears began to creep in for its continued viability. By the time of World War Two, about a quarter of Swindon's active workforce were GWR employees. As young men went into the forces, their places were taken, where appropriate, by female workers. For the duration, the works diversified, making armour plating, ammunition, explosives and timber parts for bridges. Despite this, the railway works were never bombed. Indeed, Swindon endured hostilities with fewer than 50 deaths caused by bombing and as many houses destroyed.

The Rolling Mills public house. King Street was built at right angles to Bridge Street during the 1860s. There was a beerhouse here until the middle of the 19th century, and the premises were renamed once the rail mills became established at the GWR works.

In peacetime, the workforce continued to drop, and by the late 1950s the aptly named *Evening Star* was being made; the final steam locomotive to come out of Swindon. Conversion to diesel locomotives meant that steam locomotives ceased to be built at Swindon in 1959. Ironically, the town was gearing up to celebrate 150 years of railway engineering when the works at Swindon closed in 1986. It had been a major employer to the end but, as we shall see, industrial and commercial Swindon had developed all around it. Today, the Hawksworth trading estate, the Oasis leisure centre and the North Star College occupy much of the site of the Carriage and Wagon works. The trading estate is named after Frederick William Hawksworth, a Swindon man who was the last Chief Mechanical Engineer at the GWR.

The site of other former GWR workshops became an important element in the town's regeneration for the 21st century. It took £40 million, 300 construction workers and just one year to convert buildings that included the old railway boiler shop, tank shop and smithy into BAA McArthur Glen's retail Great Western Designer Outlet Village. This upmarket regional shopping centre opened in 1997, marketed as a major tourist attraction. Close by, in the redeveloped historic complex, is the National Monuments Record's gallery and shop. The Borough of Thamesdown's 1994 Award for Conservation was given for the conversion of the GWR's offices on the railway works site, into the headquarters of the Royal Commission on the Historic Monuments of England and its picture collection.

The workers' health

As early as 1844, railway workers had formed a Locomotive & Carriage Department Sick Fund Society, mainly to provide members' sick pay. The Great Western Railway Company established its Medical Fund Society in 1847. This was a time when water for washing came out of the Wilts & Berks canal to street standpipes. Drinking water had to be carried on to the estate until the mid-1860s. The Society's solutions for public health were to develop into a blueprint for the country's National Health Service a century later. In mid-19th-century Swindon, the fledgling railway works hit its first recession; men were laid off, put on short time and found themselves unable to pay medical fees. Daniel Gooch came to an arrangement with the Board, whereby the doctor, Stuart Keith Rea, could live in one of the company's houses without rent, in return for attending works' accident victims free of charge. At the same time, workers having 'a rateable portion of their wages towards a general fund' deducted at source, could ensure they and every family member received treatment in times of illness. The workers

The GWR Railway Hospital. The wards of the hospital were a cross between a dining room and a bedroom with incredibly high ceilings. They were heated by a fireplace at each end. The photographs extant invariably show patients who are clearly well on the road to recovery, nursing staff whose starched, white pinafores were clearly something to be as proud of as any nursing skills, and equally attractive table linen. Clearly, if you were able to get out of bed, you were well enough to put on your best suit and tie for a photograph! Many of the images include men on crutches, which might suggest that injuries to the lower limbs were rather common amongst 19th-century railway workers. Certainly newspaper reports regularly referred to persons who had lost parts of their bodies, if not whole limbs, in workshop accidents. It is interesting to note how such were seen to be rather more occupational hazards than a matter for investigation and blame. Some railway companies in the 19th century had their own artificial limb-making centres, to help workers who had lost their arms or legs in accidents whilst carrying out their occupations on company premises.

subscribed, their payments defraying the cost of medicines and medical attendance, and paying the wages of the medical officer. In 1868, a series of penny readings were inaugurated at the Mechanics Institution, in order to raise some of the money that would be needed for baths. The following year, the fund provided the town's first swimming baths (open for females on Wednesday afternoons) in a small building on the north side of the railway line. Together with washing and Turkish baths, and a number of showers in Taunton Street, it all cost £800 to install.

In the matter of general health, the company was concerned insofar as an unhealthy workforce potentially affected its output. This in turn had a negative impact on profits, dividends and shareholders. Even though the company encountered a number of recessions during its first half century, it nonetheless remained in its interest to broadly support the agencies of welfare. The society itself was more concerned with the effects of poor sanitation in the railway village, than personal illness. Its officers distributed carbolic powder, chloride of lime and 'other sanitary appliances', visiting and inspecting all of the company's houses in rotation.

The Fund provided for an accident cottage hospital that was built by converting a number of Faringdon Street cottages in 1871. Initially, it had four beds for accident victims, an operating theatre, and eight beds for convalescing patients. Gradually, equipment was added; accident chairs, invalid chairs, airbeds, and a small library for the use of the patients. The hospital also subscribed to eight other public hospitals in the area, enabling some Swindon patients to be admitted elsewhere. An additional ward of six beds was added in 1898. By that time, the society's new brick building had been up for six years on the opposite side of the road. It was to have two swimming baths; the smaller was for the use of ladies and

Milton Road Baths. Built in 1892 at a cost of £10,000, the building featured two swimming baths. The larger was 111ft by 30ft in area, and was provided with an upper gallery; the smaller was 60ft by 25ft. Metal rings are still in place, on the outside wall, which allowed patrons to tether their horses. Over the years this building has been the venue for a huge range of activities including religious rallies and large dinners. Public dances were a favourite in the war years.

children, and the larger could be covered and used for dances, concerts, sales and meetings, when it might accommodate up to 2,000 people. There was also a clothing wash house that dealt with the laundry from the steadily increasing number of beds at the accident hospital, eight consulting rooms, a dental surgery and a dispensary. In 1898, this building was enlarged to include washing baths at a cost of some £5,000, and in the next year, Turkish and Russian baths were included. A hairdresser that just about saw out World War One, an ophthalmic practice, chiropody, physiotherapy and massage were amongst a whole raft of additional services introduced into this establishment right up until the mid-1940s. Two years after the National Health Service Act was passed in 1946, this building became an NHS health centre, retaining many of the Society's services. It was latterly known locally as the Milton Road Baths, and then Swindon Hydro.

The original Great Western hospital continued to be used, surrounded by flower gardens intended to assist in the recovery of patients. Even so, part of the grounds were lost to a narrow 'temporary' extension in 1927 that enabled the hospital to accommodate 42 beds, an X-ray department and a blood donor service. Nine years later, a minor accident and emergency outpatients' department with an operating theatre was installed, that continued to treat patients until the town's Princess Margaret Hospital was opened at Okus. The GWR hospital closed in 1960 and the premises became firstly, a social club for council employees, and then a community centre in 1979. Princess Margaret Hospital was erected 1957–60 to the design of Powell & Moya, and was officially opened by its namesake in 1966. In 1999, work began on its replacement at Common Head.

The 'barracks'

The railway village and works attracted a large labour force, many of whom came from the north of England. They mostly comprised single men, and the problem for the GWR was in finding somewhere they might live. The company's village quickly became overcrowded and there was very limited accommodation in Old Town. Such were the difficulties, many of these prospective workers quite quickly left the area. The GWR's solution was to use a good many of its workforce to build a large tenement structure in High Street, reputedly designed by Brunel. Initial difficulties and a recession meant that construction was not completed, and for some years the building remained empty. It seemed likely that it might become a white elephant, if not a costly ruin. Eventually it was completed at considerable expense, but again remained untenanted for a while. Finally, it was opened in 1851 as a lodging

Barracks, Faringdon Road. So great were the alterations to the GWR's lodging house, that the Wesleyan Methodists were able to claim that it had been 'erected' in 1868. The chapel itself was created by building over the space between the two lodging house wings. It had seats for up to 2,000 people, making it the largest place of worship in Swindon. At that time, the Wesleyans had two ministers living in the town. Both Revd C. Hillard and Revd Joshua Fielden were working on the Swindon circuit and offering regular services, prayer meetings and 'Sunday Schools for both sexes'.

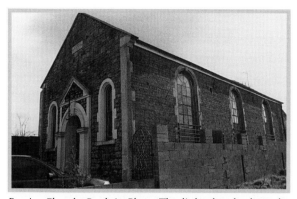

Baptist Chapel, Cambria Place. The little chapel where the services were held in their native tongue, must have been an especial haven for the Welsh workers in the GWR's rail mills. It represented the earliest Baptist presence in the new town, on land conveyed specifically for the purpose by Ambrose Lethbridge Goddard in 1864. The conveyance stipulated that the building had to be used as a Baptist chapel, and not as an inn, public house or alehouse! Also, that the outside of the building had to be painted every four years, and the inside painted or papered every seven. Although there is a date stone of 1866 on the chapel, it had actually been built (at a cost of £150) but not 'finished' by the autumn of 1865. Amongst the original trustees were occupants of Cambria Place; Robert Hill of No.29, Ebenezer Evans of No.38 (whose long association is commemorated by a plaque on the inside east wall), James Jarman who lived at No.30, and John Jarman – whose occupation was 'rougher' – from No.35. There were also Benjamin Evans, a 'baller' of 11 Westcott Street (the name given to the two sections of Cambria cottages that were put up on the line of Fleetway and Westcott Place), and Ezekiel Jones the Bridge Street tailor. The chapel was named 'Britannia Chapel' and was described as being for the use of 'Particular or Calvinistic Baptists'. It was leased to a number of tradespeople residing in Monmouthshire and Glamorgan, and Evan Thomas was its minister. Built of rock-faced limestone with Bath stone dressings, it has a very harmonious north front where two round-headed windows flank a doorway with pilasters, archivolt with keystone and pediment. Internally, with its little gallery on cast-iron columns, it could seat 150 people. The trustees had to pay one shilling per half year for 'liberty of ingress and egress with or without horses, cattle, carts or other carriages'. A schoolroom and offices were later added to the rear of the chapel. When the foundations of the schoolroom were dug up in 1996, they disclosed the body of a murder victim together with the weapon. Contemporary forensic tests were able to establish that the deed was done at least 100 years previously.

house for young, unmarried men. The building fronted the square and had two side wings to the east. Here were 100, cell-like bedrooms and communal services for cooking and laundry. It was not favoured by the occupants, and its period as a lodging house was very short; after which it once

again laid empty for several years.

In 1863, the GWR Medical Fund Society transferred the Turkish baths that they had put into the Mechanics Institution three years earlier, together with a slipper bath, to an area at the back of the barracks, that had originally been intended for use as a bakery. There were 16 baths in total, and the society also installed eight showers for the use of the residents. The bedrooms were badly converted into several-roomed apartments and let to Welsh workers in the newly opened rail mills, and their families. Even with its washing facilities, the barracks was not a success, and at one point there was an inquiry into the living conditions there. By 1864, Cambria Place was built and the Welsh families moved out of the barracks and established a community on the new estate. To begin with, the Welsh Congregationalists met in a large room behind the Greyhound public house in Cambria Place, before a little limestone Baptist chapel was put up in 1866 to serve their needs. This chapel closed in 1985.

The Wesleyan Methodists acquired the barracks, largely through the good offices of Joseph Armstrong. Until 1848, New Swindon's Wesleyans had to navigate the uphill lane to the old town in order to worship at the nearest chapel, which rapidly proved to be inadequate for their needs. That year, through the enthusiasm of Revd Aaron Langley, they acquired a small building of their own, that soon had to be enlarged. The process was repeated in 1858; a schoolroom was added, and a bigger chapel was erected. By 1863, this had once again been outgrown by its congregation, even though a gallery was added that could accommodate a further 80 worshippers. The Wesleyans bought premises in London Street from the GWR. However, the railway company decided that they wanted this for themselves, in order to expand the carriage and wagon works. They bought back the

Cambria Place has some of the most pleasing, stone faced terraces in Swindon. These were put up by a speculative builder in 1864, laid out as a mini-estate, given the Latin name for Wales (although they were known locally as 'Welsh Cottages'), and taken over by the Welsh workers at the GWR's rail mills and their families. These were the men who laboured in the hottest, noisiest part of the locomotive works. There, furnaces raged, huge steam hammers shaped white hot metal and rollers transported it through the processes. The resulting metal bars were then cut to the required lengths by means of a rotary saw. Hundreds of tons of metal were processed each week. There were ultimately to be some 48 cottages on the Cambria estate. By 1865 it comprised four blocks of back-to-back terraces with a central roadway between Westcott Street and the Wilts & Berks Canal. Originally, two smaller blocks, numbered 1-9 and 22-30 fronted the main road, with numbers 10-21 and 31-42 grouped immediately behind them. The public houses at either end appear to be integral, but this is not the case. The Grapes was put up just before the estate was built, and The Greyhound was licensed about 15 years earlier, just as nearby Westcott Place was completed. The local authority lined Cambria Place with trees in 1883.

land in a deal that included the offer of the barracks on very reasonable terms.

The Wesleyans laid a memorial stone on the site in 1868, prior to having it converted to a chapel by Thomas Barrett, to the design of Swindon architect Thomas Smith Lansdown. He changed the principal entrance from High Street (which remained unaltered) to three doorways leading on to Faringdon Street, between two 66ft-high towers. Inside these were staircases leading to the galleries overlooking the three-aisled main body of the chapel that was 69½ft wide and 88ft long. Some 1,100 people could be seated in the body of the chapel, increasing to nearly 2,000 by using the side galleries. There was a large vestibule

inside the front doors, the walls of the chapel were lined in Bath stone and the ceiling was divided into 35 panels. Outside, there were gravelled approaches surrounded by low stone walls with iron railings.

In 1962, the old barracks were fitted out as the Swindon Railway Museum, and the council allocated some of the accommodation there as flats. It remained a museum for 38 years. In 2000, its collection was transferred to STEAM – the Museum of the Great Western Railway, which HRH the Prince of Wales opened in beautifully converted railway workshops on the historic site.

The octagonal market and its successors

New Swindon was a thriving, independent community by 1853, the year in which the New Swindon Improvement Company was formed.

Market Building, High Street (now Emlyn Square). One of Swindon's great co-operative ventures had a stall in the octagonal market. The Swindon Co-operative Provident Society was established in 1850, when a group of local men distributed the profits of a box of fish by co-operative principles. They soon added flour and groceries, set up in business and established a bakery. Over the next 30 years, a number of breakaway co-operative movements came into being in the town; notably the New Swindon Industrial Co-operative Society Ltd and the Kingshill Co-operative Society. Another, formed in 1860, was the New Swindon Co-operative Provident Society whose first retail outlet was in the market. The Industrial and the Provident both subsequently opened several retail premises around the town, and their delivery vans were a familiar sight.

Commercial Road Market. Swindon's present-day, town centre 'tent-roofed' market occupies much of its original 19th-century site, after a period as a car park. In 1892, an open area of little tent-like traders' stalls was established here, surrounded by a low brick wall. The area was covered 11 years later; its multi-ridged roof supported by iron pillars and cross-braced beams. Although many Swindonians who knew the Edwardian brick building, have fond memories of it, the market hall was a lofty place that could be extremely cold, draughty and smelly. Its contemporary successor is now packed with an amazing variety of stalls, selling everything from the practical to the unusual.

This body immediately addressed the shortage of shops by planning and constructing the town's first covered general provisions market. Edward Roberts designed an octagonal building, which was built by Edward Streeter of Bath adjacent to the Mechanics Institution in the new town's High Street. The building used rough stone from the Swindon quarries for the low, surrounding wall, and had Bath stone dressings. Each side was 40ft in length between wooden corner posts. In the original plan, six of the eight sides were given a series of three windows on top of the wall, with a doorway in the other two. This would have completely enclosed the building. In the event, only the wall was built, and above it an octagonal, pointed roof of slates was supported by wooden corner posts and smaller braces between. The roof was surmounted by a round, pointed turret, supported by an openwork, wooden frame. Doorways were constructed on the north and south faces with a connecting pathway, in the centre of which played a fountain supplied with water from the railway works. Inside there were two circles of lock-ups, providing space for 32 units and 30 stalls. These were covered by canvas sheets and the woodwork throughout was of deal that had been stained and varnished.

By the time it opened, just 11 lock-ups had been taken. Five of these were leased by butchers or porkmen: John Blackford from the old town, Joseph Blackford, George Broadhurst, James Copeland and Thomas Chapman of Fleet Street.

William Stone took a stall for his boot and shoe business. J. Read sold fish, and it was reported that the stench of discarded offcuts of fish was so offensive as to be a public nuisance. B. Holmes sold tobacco, snuff and general provisions, and H. Wilson had general provisions for sale. There was also the Ready-Made-Clothes Depot and general drapery warehouse, and a Mr Williams had a greengrocery stall.

A minor hiatus occurred in 1855 when it was discovered that the New Swindon Improvement Company actually had no right to take the tolls from traders in the market. The licence to do so had been granted to Ambrose Lethbridge Goddard, Lord of the Manor, when he last renewed his Old Swindon market rights. Faced with a potential loss, the Improvement Company quickly agreed terms. Whilst these problems were being thrashed out, the GWR was involved in difficult – and ultimately fruitless – discussions with Ambrose Lethbridge Goddard, because they wanted to establish their own cattle market in a field adjacent to the Queen's Tap. However, it was Old Swindon's William Dore who eventually succeeded. In 1860, he began holding sales on a private ground near the Queen's Hotel at the station, on non-market days to avoid paying market tolls. The GWR had clearly missed that particular loophole!

During the 1860s, the New Swindon Industrial Co-operative Society rented its first retail outlet in the High Street market building. Trade was clearly promising enough for the Society to invest in its own premises in 1874. Yet two years later, their stores for the supply of bread, flour, grocery, drapery, etc. in East Street, received a mixed review. According to one commentator, the enterprise paid satisfactory dividends to the promoters but 'the co-operative principle has not accomplished at Swindon what might have been expected in a community almost entirely of working men in

possession of weekly paid wages, and, consequently, able to pay cash and gain the advantage of the dividend arising from co-operation'.

Because of the market building and the ad hoc trading that took place outside it, this part of New Swindon's High Street became known as Market Square. Travelling vendors set up open stalls in the surrounding square on Fridays, later lighting their wares by naptha lamps. On other occasions, sales of livestock took place around the market. The area became a haunt of cheapjacks and quack doctors. The children who played in and around the building during the day, returned at night, attracted by the bartering and the lights.

Before it was closed down in 1872, a ramshackle, wooden, beer house, known as the Engineers' Arms (or the Hole in the Wall after its method of dispensing off-sales), was attached to the market building. The area declined generally, and within a couple of decades the market house had become neglected and in a poor state. By 1880, it had been pronounced a public nuisance. All trade inside it stopped. The market building became a children's playground, tramps slept there, the woodwork rotted and the masonry crumbled. In 1891, it was demolished to facilitate an extension to the Mechanics Institution. In 1900, the area adjacent to the Mechanics Institution, including the site of the former market building, was renamed Emlyn Square.

As for the market rights, they had been transferred to the New Swindon Local Board in 1890. The Board negotiated land for their own open market on an extensive, triangular island site beside the canal bridge in Commercial Road. Designed by H.J. Hamp, it opened for trading in 1892, with 17 'shops' and a triangular area which accommodated numerous stalls. Eleven years later, the sides were built up into a great flight of gables, and the interior was roofed on metal piers and supports, all at a cost of about £5,000. A grand, pedimented entrance of red brick with stone dressings faced defiantly up Commercial Road, and was eventually distinguished by its incredibly intricate, wrought-iron gates. This site was acquired by Swindon Corporation in 1903. The main area had an annexed fish market, used as a fire engine depot between 1941 and 1959, and subsequently a cut price sale room. It was all closed down in 1977 and such market traders as were able and willing, were transferred to a market hall in the Brunel Shopping Centre that had been completed the year before. The 1903 building was demolished and was, for a while, a car park until a new covered market was put up in 1995, when the traders re-occupied their old site. At the same time, the Brunel Centre underwent a major extension and refurbishment programme.

Trip holidays

No aspect of life in Swindon occasioned more comic postcards, mostly badly drawn and today of almost unfathomable humour, than the GWR trip holiday. In 1849, some members of the Mechanics Institution went on an unpaid day trip to Oxford, on a train provided free by the Company. This led to an annual 'trip' day which always took place on the first Friday in July; within a decade or so there was a choice of venues. The 'trip' days were the forerunners of an unpaid week's holiday in 1913 (then suspended until 1919) and then the annual holiday in July when the railway works closed down for ten days.

The night before the trip, the head of the household, if not the whole family, usually had an unscheduled bath. Most people walked to town on the trip days, and were marshalled into special trains drawn up in the carriage sidings near Sheppard Street. There they were packed into compartments in much the same way as we are

today, at rush hour on the London underground, and conveyed to seaside resorts whose landladies usually met the trains and touted for business. At its height, the trains left at 15 minute intervals, after which Swindon became almost as a ghost town for the duration. It was said that when they arrived at their destinations, the women and children went on to the beach, whilst the men spent their days in the public houses. There was, however, the ever-present problem of finance. The breadwinners of those families that could not afford more than a day or two away, often took part-time jobs to fill in the rest of the week and make a little money. For most people, the holiday was a mixed blessing, in that it gave them a break but caused money worries. Several of those old postcards show queues of tradesmen attempting unsuccessfully to extract payment of their bills in the weeks following the trip.

The ever status-conscious GWR allocated a number of free passes annually, dependent on each employee's position at the works. At other times, rail travel was available to employees at a heavily discounted rate. Swindon's shops normally closed early on Wednesdays. When there was a significant increase in the number of families leaving the town for several days during the annual shutdown of the railway works, many with the aid of moneylenders, the shops closed all day on Wednesdays. The GWR provided its first paid week's holiday for employees in 1938, and increased this to two weeks, ten years later. The workers also benefited from cheap coal and wood (known locally as 'the allocation'), the latter including whole railway sleepers.

St Mark's Church

Before St Mark's Church was built, the railway company provided a venue for Anglican worship. Lt Col Thomas Vilett owned the land to the west

St Mark's Church, Park Lane. The impact of Revd the Hon J.M.G. Ponsonby's incumbency (1879–1903) on the parish of St Mark was considerable. Of a titled family, into which he was to succeed, Ponsonby (later a Canon of Bristol Cathedral) was responsible for a great spiritual resurgence in the parish. He also created the parish of St Paul to meet the spiritual needs of the old area of Eastcott, and a mission that held services at different times and in several locations to be more convenient to the worshippers. He was also the catalyst for the creation of St Saviour's Church which the railway workers built in 1889, and subsequently enlarged. In 1855, St Mark's bought a new organ, and the old one was purchased for the Mechanics Institution theatre where it was put into the service of the musical entertainments.

St Augustine's Church, Summers Street. In the decade or so after 1880, a whole series of streets were put in north of the GWR main line, in the angle formed by the branch line to Gloucester. The Rodbourne Road became the artery from which a number of speculative builders laid out roads, from Redcliffe Street to Hughes Street, and named most of them after themselves. St Augustine's was opened in 1908 when the district of Rodbourne, that had previously devolved on parts of St Mark's and Rodbourne Cheney, became a separate ecclesiastical parish.

St Luke's Church, Broad Street. At the beginning of the 20th century, lowland Swindon was expanding eastwards across the fields towards the County Ground. Manchester Road had recently been extended, and a large area of land bounded by the canal to the south, and County Road to the east, had recently come on the market. Broad Street was put in parallel to Manchester Road in 1901, and over 1,200 new houses were planned in terraces on a grid system based on these two thoroughfares. A church was built in 1903 to support the new community. This is now the church hall, and next to it stands St Luke's; designed by W.A.H. Masters and opened in 1912. It features a strange, crocketted bellcote and a castellated façade with some 14th-century-style windows.

St Barnabas's Church, Gorse Hill. Under a Local Government Board Order, Gorse Hill was amalgamated with the parish of Swindon in 1890. The ecclesiastical parish of St Barnabas was formed there from part of the parish of Stratton St Margaret. J.P. Seddon of Westminster designed the church in 13th-century style. It was built of Swindon stone, cost £3,200 and was opened in 1885. Until 1894, when the south aisle and vestries were added, it comprised only a clerestoried nave of six bays that could seat 370 people, a chancel, and a central turret with a single bell. These additions cost £900. The adjacent Sunday school building and concert hall, was designed by local architect John J. Smith. The nearby vicarage, built in 1892, cost £2,000. An intended tower that is now the south porch, was built in 1912.

of that acquired from J.H. Sheppard for the railway village, and gave a portion of it as the site for St Mark's. The firm of George Gilbert Scott & W.B. Moffat submitted the design, as they also did for the nearby vicarage, school and schoolhouse. The church and school were built in 1845 and the first vicar was Revd Joseph Mansfield. The former's cost of £6,000 was defrayed by a bequest under the will of a GWR executive, and an amount of private funding. St Mark's was designed in Decorated style, although its cluster columns have an earlier feel. The tower with its 140ft high, ribbed and crocketted broach spire is to the north-west of the church, where it could be viewed to best advantage by railway travellers. Until 1846, the parish was under the jurisdiction of Old Swindon; then it became a parish in its own right. The school lasted for 34 years, by which time children's education in Swindon, including that at the GWR-sponsored College Street School of 1873, had been invested in a School Board.

The Park, Faringdon Road. The 190 men of the 11th (Wilts) New Swindon Rifle Corps, under Major W.F. Gooch, formerly had an armoury in Taunton Street, in the railway village; surely a matter of some disquiet to the residents. However, the Corps had a fine, 22-man band under the direction of William Hawkins, that doubtless gave them considerable entertainment. In 1871, an 8,000 sq.ft. drill hall was built for the Rifle Corps 'in the cricket field and near St Mark's Church' (where the Territorial Army premises now stand on the corner of Church Place and Rodbourne Road). The cost of £1,500 was mostly defrayed by the GWR company. This annexed area of the park was immediately screened off with foliage. For a while, the drill hall had to accommodate female pupils, as an overspill schoolroom. To the north of this building, set back into the shrubbery on the Park Lane side, there was a cricket pavilion. The field itself was an oval, surrounded by a walkway with seats (some 20 in all) placed at regular intervals. All of the formal and ornamental gardens were concentrated around the main entrance from Church Place, through which gateway the area of grass was set off by a large, colourful island bed. To the left of the entrance was the park lodge house, on either side of which were formally laid out gardens with fountains. When all of this was done, Park Lane, which was to become a tree-lined road of fine terraced houses on the tramcar route to Rodbourne terminus, had not been built up. Only one dwelling, Courts Knapp Cottage, existed in its own grounds close to the junction with Westcott Place.

The Park

In 1844, land to the east of the emerging railway village was purchased from Lt Col Vilett for use as a cricket ground. A permanent pavilion was installed and the New Swindon cricket team played there from 1867. Meanwhile, in 1866, the Mechanics Institution held their inaugural children's fete on the site with all manner of

events, attractions and amusements. This must have been the largest gathering of youngsters and their parents in the history of the new town, and certainly the happiest. The juvenile fete, held in August, went annually from strength to strength and, except for the years of World War One, continued until 1939. For a while too, a little bandstand stood on the green. By the turn of the 20th century, the park was a general pleasure

Park Lane on the west side of the GWR
pleasure ground.

Park House, Church Place. Originally called Park Road, the name reflected the attractive outlook of this one-sided street, whose houses had an unhindered view of the GWR pleasure ground. They would have overlooked fine, ornamental greenhouses and splendid, semi-formal Victorian borders of herbaceous plants and annuals that were much in vogue at the time. Park House, the largest of the buildings in this street, is a three-storey, gabled house of 1876. It is remarkably elegant and well proportioned for Swindon, built of brick with stone dressings and having a substantial porch. The GWR Medical Fund Society rented it in 1908 as a home for some of its medical staff, and it later became the company's medical headquarters.

Rodbourne Road, also known as Rodbourne Lane, ran from the railway bridge at the end of Park Lane to Bruce Street bridge; close by the terminus for the Rodbourne arm of the tramway. It was part of a trackway that ultimately linked the road to Wootton Bassett with Rodbourne Cheney. Although when built up, it too was partly tree-lined, Rodbourne Road never aspired to the status of Park Lane. On the west side were tightly packed streets of small terraces, convenient homes for the railway workers who approached the works through the Rodbourne Road entrance. Small shops were put into the residential terraces on Rodbourne Road, particularly near the tram terminus and the GWR work's gate. These facilitated the growing community and the daily needs of the workers. Inextricably bound up in all of this was the Dolphin public house of 1873, whose first landlord was Robert Bishop, later to be in charge of the Great Western Hotel.

ground, bounded by formal ornamental gardens and freely patronised by all. It remained under the control of the Institution's Park Improvement Committee until taken over by Swindon Corporation as a public park in 1925.

The early spread of New Swindon

Long before the railway village was completed, private builders began speculative developments outside it. Workers' houses were put up comfortably close, along and off a track known as Fleetway. This ran south of the railway village, linking with the road from Old Swindon to Wootton Bassett, and was to be designated Westcott Place in 1845. Almost immediately it included a number of traders. Butcher John

No Swindon thoroughfare was given over to commerce and trade as rapidly as Regent Street. Two decades after the railway came to the town, only a few little terraces of one-up-one-down cottages, a handful of single buildings and the occasional front room shop, were to be encountered between the Wilts & Berks Canal and the Rifleman's Arms public house. By the 1890s, the whole street had been transformed. Few of the original buildings had not been given over to business at street level, and some had already been enhanced by custom-built, typical Victorian traders' frontages. The street was packed with such properties on both sides. Many of the spaces between the groups of original houses were being filled by larger business premises, some three-storeys high and many individually designed. Regent Street, by the latter 1890s, was in every way superior to trading areas of the old town.

Blackford opened his first New Swindon shop here, as did John Carpenter the chandler and coal carrier. There also, were to be found William Smith, William Stone, James Toe and John Millard the boot and shoe makers; the entrepreneurial grocer, baker and ironmonger John Martin; William Hassall the furniture broker; and beer retailers Henry Cross, and Tobias Hurcomb who was also a tailor.

In about 1842, 12 canal workers' cottages were put up on the Wilts & Berks Canal, a little to the south-east, and named Cetus Buildings, together with the Whale beer house. Station Road was so called in 1843 and a number of informal dwellings were built adjacent to the village. By 1848 the new town had an estimated population of about 2,500, roughly equal to that in the town on the hill. A few dwellings were put up near the north end of what became Bridge Street, and were called Sheppard's Cottages after J.H.H. Sheppard who owned the land next to the railway village. These predated Sheppard Street, built and so named at his request, 25 years later.

In 1855, Bridge Street came into being, marking the north-east boundary of the railway village and at the same time starting a route that would eventually link up with Victoria Street in Old Swindon. For the next 22 years, the whole of this track on both sides of the canal was known as Bridge Street. The northern end of Bridge Street, which stretched between Fleet Street and the railway line, very quickly changed from residential cottages to small trading premises which provided products and services for the railway workers. Around these traders, a small, fairly self-contained community gradually built up in the red brick houses adjacent to the railway village, but not exactly part of it. By the end of the century, there were, within a few yards of each other in Bridge Street, a cycle repair shop, shoe repairer (both very important to the railway workers), barber,

tobacconist, pork butcher, faggot and peas shop, grocer, sweet shop and restaurant. It was here, in 1919, that Samuel Gray bought a small bakery in a two-bedroom cottage and set to work in it with his son Cyril. At the time, there were 30 other small bakeries operating in the town, but being so close to the railway workshops, this one had the edge. Samuel gradually bought up adjacent Bridge Street cottages and outbuildings, and the business expanded. Gray's was to become the most enduring bakery in Swindon, having seven retail outlets by 1940. Cyril Gray retired from the business in 1998, aged 92.

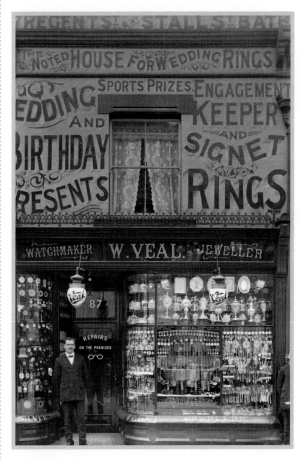

When the whole of the lane from Fleet Street to Upper Eastcott Farm was one, there was already one refreshment stop on the way. A few hundred yards to the south of Fleet Street was the Wilts & Berks canalside Golden Lion Inn, built

Regent Street, 1890.

Regent Street. A typical mid-Victorian terrace, before it was converted to trade.

The face of Regent Street had completely changed by the early years of the 20th century.

Opening sale in 1901 at Keogh Bros. 45 Bridge Street.

c.1845, which already had a cluster of cottages about it. There were new buildings too, on the track leading up through Eastcott, not too far from the ancient cottages associated with Old Town. By the end of the 1840s, a Methodist Chapel had been erected in some isolation on this route.

The new town may have developed at a faster rate, had it not been for a recession at the railway works late in the 1840s. This appears to have slowed down building in the railway village itself, and undoubtedly had a temporary effect on speculative building outside. However, it did not deter investment in public houses. For well over a decade, an isolated beer house called the Greyhound had stood on the trackside of what was to become Fleetway. Along the road to

Wootton Bassett, William Brooks had the Running Horse which opened in the mid-1820s, where once there had been Ladd's Mill. By 1850, thirsty railway workers could find satisfaction at the Golden Lion run by John Cross, or they might drink with James W. Bannister at the Ship which had been part of the 1840s development in Westcott Place. The Falcon was to open there in 1849, and the Duke of York in 1851. The town's three 'Queen's' hostelries were centred around the station: James Davies' Arms, and the Hotel and the Tap which were both run by J.R. Phillips.

The railway village's public houses continued to thrive. In 1850 there were also 13 beer retailers listed at New Swindon. Some of these beer house owners had named premises; for example, George Bishop who had opened the George on the road

50 Regent Street, *c.*1910. The business closed in 1968.

47 Regent Street, showing Mr Sparkes' delivery team.

through Eastcott in 1847, was also to open the Lamb and Flag in Bridge Street in 1854. The Engineers' Arms arrived south-east of the station in 1841, the Locomotive appeared in Fleetway in 1846 and another Greyhound the following year. In 1850, a beer house called the Jolly Sailor opened in Bridge Street. The position of these public houses demonstrates how New Swindon grew in the couple of decades following the coming of the railway company's works.

As the 1860s approached, the population of New Swindon topped the 4,000 mark. Houses were built immediately south-east of the railway village in 1850, and five years later, King Street and Queen Street were developed each side of northern Bridge Street. During the same decade, houses began to appear along the trackway between Fleetway and Eastcott. The next residential push was to expand the town southwards by means of terraces along Bridge Street towards Regent's Place. Here went in Albion Terrace, Waterloo Terrace, Alma Terrace and Bellwood Place. Shops soon began to establish in this area.

By 1865, there were a fair number of workmen's cottages south of the canal, terminating in the newly opened Rifleman's Arms at the Eastcott Farm end. In 1866 and 1867, Cromwell Street and Havelock Street were built into the fields immediately south of the canal, and linked by Brunel Street. As these were being planned, so too was a development near the top of Eastcott Lane, close to Bath Road. Before the decade finished, North Street, East Street and Lansdown Road formed a residential oasis close to the old town. The main thoroughfare north of the Golden Lion Bridge was designated Regent Street from 1867 which, particularly after the Golden Lion had gone and the canal had been filled in, left an apparently illogical junction between this and Bridge Street.

Cromwell Street was probably begun in the 1860s; one of the earliest to be built off the developing Regent Street. Ultimately, it linked with Commercial Road where the town's open air market was established in 1892. At the Regent Street end it was hardly discernible from the shops in the main thoroughfare, but gradually became a street of terraced houses and small traders. Hooper photographers is shown at 6 Cromwell Street (above) c.1912, and (below) previously at 2 Market Street.

The 1870s began with a residential extension to the east of the railway village – Henry Street, Harding Street and Sheppard Street – on land acquired from John Harding Sheppard. John Street was developed to the south, terminating in a bridge where the Wilts & Berks Canal and the North Wilts Canal met. It was said that a person standing in about 1840, in the allotment gardens between the end of Victoria Street and Prospect in Old Swindon, looking down the hillside and over the lowlands, would have seen only some 20 or 30 dwellings in the whole panorama, and not all of these were occupied. By the early 1870s, there were more than 1,700 inhabited buildings in the

Catalogue Houses, Drove Road. The brick and tile works connected with the clay pits that are now part of Queen's Park ornamental gardens, were probably opened in the 18th century. A 19th-century head of the family firm was Thomas Turner. He lived nearby at the Grove (now a restaurant) and fronted his yard with his 'catalogue houses', originally named 'Pottery Cottages'. These were built to advertise the bricks, finials, mouldings and other terracotta decorative motifs that were available at his Swindon Tile & Pottery Works. Amongst the items for sale were flower pots, rustic armchairs, 'elegantly moulded tablets', ornamental pottery and all kinds of ware adapted for domestic use. Turner supplied bricks for many of the houses that were to link the old and new towns, some still distinguishable by his characteristic 'TT' initialled date stones. His bricks also went into the bank building on the corner of Wood Street and Cricklade Street, and enlargements to buildings on the Marlborough College campus. He was also proprietor of similar brickworks at Stratton, and at both premises prided himself on their cleanliness, and welcomed visitors. Turner had interests at Swindon Wharf on the Wilts & Berks Canal, and was latterly a director of the company. Turner Street (1893) is named after him.

same landscape. Some of these were on the 300-house estates that included the eastern sections of Albion Street, Radnor Street and William Street, immediately south of the Wilts & Berks Canal. By the late 1870s, there were 66 named streets either completed or in development in New Swindon.

For the first few decades, the inhabitants of New Swindon relied on the shops and service businesses in the old town. As the second half of the 19th century progressed, Old Swindon residents came down the hill to patronise the growing number of retail shops in Westcott Place and along the line of Bridge Street and Regent Street. The number of shops and variety of traders in Regent Street began to increase dramatically, and by the 1870s, this had become the main shopping centre. Here too, the vogue for coffee houses was established. The Kooloo Coffee House was at 36 Bridge Street and the Swindon Coffee Palace Company arrived in Regent Street in 1880 to 'give the Swindon public the option of refreshment dissociated from intoxicants'. It opened the Three Cups coffee house with its 'commodious bar and club rooms'.

Hand-in-hand with the builders were the building societies, in particular the Swindon Permanent Benefit Building and Investment Society. In 1876 this was said to have been 'the means of covering acres of land with substantial houses (209 to date), chiefly for the artisan population'. The Oxford Society, Reading Society, Wilts & Western and the Ramsbury Building Society were also financing much of New Swindon at this time. Old and New Swindon continued to grow together physically, with New Swindon's private developers looking to the old landowning families to sell their holdings of land. This was much needed for further expansion, in order to accommodate a new town population that was just under 12,000 in 1871, increased to 15,000 by the end of the next decade, and topped 27,000 at the 1891 census.

The great breakthrough as regards land development came in 1885, when the Rolleston estate, that had come down through the Vilett family, was finally freed from litigation in chancery. This enabled a large area to the west of

Central Club and Institution, Commercial Road. Arguably always the most imposing of the working mens' clubs, this three-storey building of red brick with Bath stone dressings was designed by R.J. Beswick, erected in 1897 and cost £6,500. It made the most of its elevated position next to the Milton Road bridge of the Wilts & Berks Canal (and the fine baluster parapet of the bridge) by incorporating covered access alongside the waterway. At the time, neo-Dutch renaissance style was favoured for the town's more important buildings, after the precedent set by the Town Hall. The club's round-headed, shoulder pediment on the south front – although a restrained example – exemplified this. The feature was to be seen at its most exuberant on the Queen's Theatre, with which the Central Club was an exact contemporary, and a few years later on the nearby market hall. It also had a stone porch with a strange, triangular pediment. The porch was picked out in coloured lights when the building was used as a discotheque in the 1960s and 70s. In its days as a club, it had a reading room, concert hall, billiard room and double skittle alley. The building was demolished in 1982.

the developing town to become available for expansion. Former farm land parallel with Regent Street was built up from c.1890, and over the next few years, numerous terraces comprising hundreds of red brick houses appeared. The area between York Square (the temporary name then given to the space adjacent to York Terrace and soon to become Regent Circus) and Faringdon Street was the first to benefit. Commercial Road was completed with houses and shops. It converged with Regent Street on York Place to the east, and a new canal bridge was built at the other end to access Faringdon Street. The last 15 years of the 19th century saw the wholesale colonisation of what is now central Swindon, the area bounded by the line of the Wilts & Berks Canal to the north, and Bath Road/The Sands to the south. These were row after row of brick terraces, gobbling up former gardens and allotments, to lay out central Swindon as it is today. Tightly packed railway

Cheltenham Street, Niblett & Co. The Swindon Permanent (Benefit) Building (and Investment) Society was formed in 1868 and had its offices in the Mechanics Institution. Its officers could hardly have had a more impeccable pedigree; Daniel Gooch was the president, and amongst its directors were William Brewer Wearing, manager of the County of Gloucester Bank, and Lyttleton Etty who was to succeed him in 1881. There were also John Chandler the Wood Street draper and William Vaughan Edwards the ironmonger. The latter's Castle Iron Works foundry was reached off Wood Street next to the King's Arms inn. One of the first investments made by this Society was the purchase of land in 1869, in the triangle formed at New Swindon by the railway line to the north, the Wilts & Berks Canal to the south and the North Wilts branch. Here they laid out about 150 buildings comprising Cheltenham Street, Gloucester Street and Wellington Street. Each of them became known for corner buildings. Cheltenham Street was home to Niblett's water company in the last couple of decades of the 1800s; Gloucester Street had Tunley's artists' materials shop that still exists, not far from its original location. Wellington Street was demolished to make way for the town's bus station. Only the northern sections of these three streets survive.

workers' cottages spread towards Rodbourne and Cheney Manor. As the century ended, the most rapid growth was taking place north of the railway line, towards Gorse Hill.

Hand-in-hand with all of this residential expansion came a rush of school building during the last two decades of the 19th century. College Street School was built by the GWR in 1873 and leased to the Swindon School Board. Then, in fairly rapid succession, Sanford Street, Westcott, Clifton Street and Clarence Street schools

appeared before the end of the century. After Jennings Street and Clarence Street schools were built in the first years of the 20th century, there was a lull in school building in central Swindon. The emphasis gradually shifted to the developing areas and the peripheral settlements that were being established. Some of these schools were associated with the old villages that were being developed as part of the overall urban plan, such as Moredon and Rodbourne, and other schools were being built – as at Pinehurst and Penhill – to

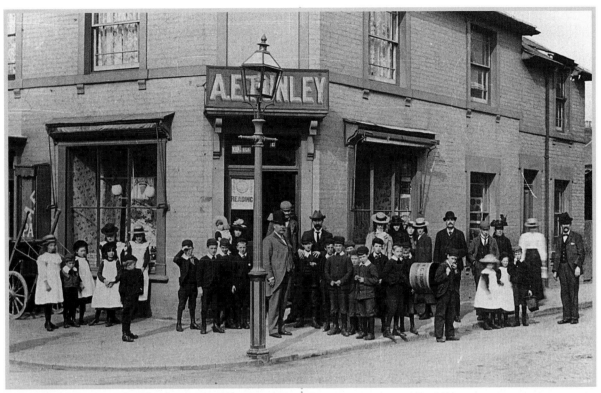

Milford Street. This is an example of an undistinguished street, just on the outskirts of retail development, that still exists but has completely lost its identity. Its residents had to cross a little bridge over the North Wilts Canal to get to the shopping centre. From 1903 until 1979, when it was destroyed by fire, a timber-framed and panelled Railway Mission on the corner with Wellington Street, provided for the spiritual needs of railwaymen.

accommodate children from the new estates. Even Headlands Grammar School, opened as late as 1952, right on Swindon's boundary with Stratton St Margaret, took many of its '11 plus' examination successes from the newly developing areas of its satellite neighbour.

The Ship, Westcott Place. This substantial building dates from the early 1890s. Its origins lie in an adjacent house where Elizabeth Cave carried on the occupation of beer retailer throughout the 1840s and 1850s. By the close of the former, her premises had been named the Ship, licensed to James William Bannister, and in 1869 the landlord was George Smith. It came to public notice in 1903 when barmaid Hettie Swinford was shot in the chest, in the bar parlour of the hotel. Her murderer was Edward Richard Palmer, a former GWR labourer with whom she had at sometime almost contracted marriage. After a period away from the town, Palmer had gone to the public house and carried out the murder after spending time with friends at the nearby Mechanics Institution.

The 1870s and 1880s saw the development of yet another 'village', immediately to the south-east of the station towards the company's brickworks; a finger of terraced streets following the railway line to London. By the turn of the century, another finger had run south, past Eastcott Farm, to the little hump-backed Whale Bridge where the bargees' cottages and Medgbury Road backed on to the tow path of the Wilts & Berks Canal. Until the late 1880s, the north-eastern part of Princes Street, admitting on to the Whale Bridge, was not built up. There was a large square of open land to the east of the street, adjacent to brickworks with their associated clay pits and kilns. After that, the

area was uninhabited up to Swindon Wharf, and beyond that was almost entirely open countryside.

The Swindon Brick & Tile Works opened beside the Wilts & Berks Canal in the 1870s, and was a wonder of the age in Swindon, largely because the proprietors had paid a lot of money to secure sole rights for the use of Mr Hoffman's Patent Brick Kiln, and were at great pains to explain how it worked. Clay was brought up in trucks from the surrounding pits and shaped in brick-making machines, powered by a 20

South-west new town, from Okus. In 1900, none of the streets in this photograph existed. In the foreground and background there were allotments, and in the middle distance would have been the chimney and kilns of the Bath Road Brick Works. To the west there was a cluster of buildings that comprised the hamlet of Okus, all surrounded by fields and crossed by a network of tracks. In the distance, the Wilts & Berks Canal could be glimpsed as far as the King's Hill bridge, and it might even have been possible to make out the Running Horse public house on the Wootton Bassett Road. At that time, the new town extended only to the north side of King's Hill Road. Grosvenor Road was the first to go in just before World War One, but building hereabouts was not resumed until the 1930s.

horsepower steam engine. Each of these machines could press the clay, work it, and shape and cut up to 20,000 bricks per day. The public were expected to grasp the significance of a system that saved at least 6cwt of coal on every 1,000 bricks made. This was a 12-chamber kiln which took three million bricks (made on site) to build, arranged in a circle around a chimney shaft. The kiln was lined with firebricks that cost £1,000. Once bricks had been shaped, they would

Rifleman's Arms Hotel, Regent Street. The present fabric is the result of rebuilding in 1888, when the public house was around 35 years old. It originally occupied a substantial, wedge-shaped plot with outbuildings set well back from the road, and stabling at the rear next to York Place. Access to the stables was directly off Regent Street, through a walled stable courtyard. Prior to the rebuilding, the inn presented a flat façade to the roadway. Both of the wings on the present structure are much later additions. One of the most significant events to take place there was the first meeting of the Swindon & District Trades Council in 1891.

traditionally have been dried in the open air before firing; an impossibility in wet weather. Mr Hoffman's kiln complex allowed for a huge, roofed upper room where drying could take place, and through which the kilns were fed with coal. By the mid-1870s, the company was firing upwards of 150,000 bricks at a single burning. Smaller kilns on the site made pottery, roofing and fancy tiles, vases and garden containers. Even then, residential Swindon was beginning to close in.

Spring Gardens was built off Princes Street in 1888, along the southern edge of this land. This was the catalyst for completing the north-east side of Princes Street with a residential terrace towards the bridge. This ended in a new Wesleyan Mission Hall set back from the road. In 1893, Ernest Clement Skurray built a four-storey

flour mill (Town Flour Mill), offices and outbuildings on a substantial site on the south bank of the canal, just behind the Mission Hall. The mill, which operated until 1924 when it was substantially demolished, had its own canalside wharf for receiving deliveries of corn, and exporting flour. In 1899, Skurray bought his first motor car and thereafter combined the businesses of miller and motor engineer. Traces of the mill remained until 1964.

The garage side of the business was taken over by H.C. Praeter in 1934, and the strange Princes Street showroom frontage – an open pediment flanked by ogee-shaped mouldings descending to ball finials on pillars – remained a landmark building at the Whale Bridge. (Its other landmark building was a little square, cast-iron, 19th-century gentlemen's urinal.) Skurray transferred his motor interests to the former Deacon & Liddiard's Vale of the White Horse Repository, beside Manchester House in High Street, Old

Freeth's of Fleet Street. Fleet Street was the link between the railway village and the developing new town, in particular the shopping centre that was growing up from the mid-1800s along the line of Bridge Street and Regent Street. H.F. Freeth was clearly at pains to show that here was a class establishment, well run with a considerable staff and a good stock. This must have been in sharp contrast to the experience of the older members of the community who would have recalled the state of some butchers' shops in the old town, and later, that of meat sellers in the High Street covered market in the railway village.

Swindon. This was a typical, three-storey Georgian tenement that had been converted to offices. Skurray's retained this arrangement, putting their workshops into the outbuildings at the rear. The Georgian building was pulled down in 1927 and the whole frontage rebuilt in mock Tudor style to incorporate a garage entrance and showrooms. Sadly, a whole cluster of 19th-century stone buildings were destroyed on the corner of Newport Street and High Street in the late 1960s, when Skurray's expanded. The mock Tudor frontage remained until the company removed to Drove Road (not far from where they began) in 1984. The old town premises were demolished and the Co-op store and car park now occupy the whole of Deacon & Liddiard's and Skurray's extension sites.

The other railway line

One of the great local debates in the late 1870s was the intention to connect Swindon, by a narrow gauge railway, with Andover via Marlborough, possibly continuing to Southampton. Lord Ernest Bruce ceremonially started the work at Marlborough in 1875. The Swindon, Marlborough & Andover Railway Company estimated that it would take about two and a half years to cover the 33 miles, ultimately connecting with the GWR line, east of Swindon station. The original proposals for the Swindon section included constructing a tunnel some 830 yards long beneath Old Swindon. This proved to be too expensive and alternative routes were considered. For several reasons, it was 1877 before the project was up and running. The first section of line, between Swindon and Marlborough opened in 1881.

Ambrose Lethbridge Goddard was deputy-chairman of the concern, and Swindon solicitor John Coplestone Townsend acted for the railway company. In the event, after leaving Swindon

(Old) Town Station south of Newport Street, the Midland & South Western Junction Railway's line curved westwards and on to Rushey Platt, after which it slipped into the GWR line at Mannington Bridge, west of Swindon Station. In 1883, the Swindon & Cheltenham Extension Railway line was opened from Rushey Platt to Cricklade and Cirencester, and the GWR opened a branch from Swindon to Highworth, with an interim station near Kingsdown.

As for the M&SWJ railway line, it was never particularly successful or approved of by the GWR, only insofar as it provided a certain amount of additional passenger and freight traffic on the main line. The old town's station was famed for its attractive gardens at the Newport Street approach. In 1894, a licence was granted for its refreshment rooms. These continued – known locally as the 'ghost train' – for four years after passenger services finished in 1961. The line had been taken over by the GWR in 1923. The area of the old town station is now a residential and business development, and the bed of the railway line is a designated cycle route which will eventually link up with cycleways on Swindon's planned northern residential development.

Electricity and tramways

Somewhere between the long-distance coaches and the horse-drawn carriages that conveyed the public around the town, were the carriers who operated between Swindon and the nearby villages. Hawkins' *The Old Firm* for example, that ran between the town and Wroughton, began as a horse drawn passenger carrier in 1870, and later ran its own motor buses until the mid-1950s. There were others too, who operated out of the crossroads which were to become the tram centre. Gilling's horse and brake, was one example, in which it was possible to go via Rodbourne to the

Swindon's tram routes centred on the point at which Bridge Street met Fleet Street. By the end of the 19th century, the former had become a retail centre leading into Regent Street, and the latter was no less a centre for trade. Here was Clappen's Corner where William Clappen had his business as a tailor and outfitter, opposite the Volunteer public house. The main tram route which ran between the old town Market Place and Gorse Hill, followed that previously taken by Kembrey's horse-drawn carriers. The tram drivers took their departure times off the Centre from Mr Clappen's clock, put up c.1880, which became a landmark in this part of the town. The clock and premises were taken over by shoe retailer Stead & Simpson, who entered into an agreement which allowed the Corporation to maintain the clock and keep it accurate, so the trams ran on time. It was converted to electricity in 1938. Next door to William Clappen was Samuel Smith, chemist and sub-postmaster. The New Swindon Post Office remained as an annexe to this shop until 1900, when it was replaced in Regent Circus.

Duke of Edinburgh public house in Gorse Hill, for one penny. Another carrier was Cullern who provided a regular horse drawn service between Gorse Hill, New Swindon and the old town.

Electrification of Swindon and the establishment of tramways went hand in hand. In the early 1880s, the new Swindon Local Board was approached by interested electric lighting companies, and there were various proposals for a public steam tramway system. (Steam buses had been operating in Britain since the early 1830s.) One of these proposals, made in 1883, suggested a permanent route between the Market Square in the old town and the GWR station. Electricity first came to the town under the Swindon New Town Electric Lighting Order, 1895, and the dual public

service was the result of the Swindon Corporation Tramways & Electricity Bill, 1901. The Council formed an Electric Light & Tramways Committee, and Lower Eastcott Farm was purchased. The farmland had shrunk considerably and built-up terraces now abutted it on all sides, although the roadside stone buildings remained, the last integrated farmstead of its type in Swindon. A.J. Colbourne built the local authority's electricity works there, an austere structure with a 150ft landmark chimney and a cooling tower that was later to be rebuilt at Moredon.

The electricity works opened in 1903. A proposal for 8 miles of track having been rejected, work immediately began on digging up certain thoroughfares to accommodate 3½ miles of 42-

inch track. This would ultimately connect Old Swindon's Market Place with a terminus at the junction of Bridge Street and Fleet Street, after which extensions led into Rodbourne and Gorse Hill. There was also to be a spur between Wellington Street and the GWR station. A shed was built adjacent to the electricity works to accommodate the tramcars, ultimately 13 of them over the period of the undertaking, numbered and painted in cream and crimson lake. The system was inaugurated by the mayor, James Hinton, in September 1904.

Corporation Electricity Showrooms. By the time Swindon Corporation put up its art deco showrooms, Regent Circus was being modernised all round.

Trams became an extremely popular, but latterly not particularly profitable, method of travel in Swindon, despite an accident that occurred on 1 June 1906. A packed car, descending Victoria Road, gathered speed and overturned on a curve at the foot of the hill. Five deaths resulted, and more than 30 people were injured. It transpired that the tram had been allowed to continue despite a reported problem with the brake mechanism. Special rates had to be levied in Swindon over the next three years to meet the substantial compensation claims against the Corporation.

Meanwhile, the electricity undertaking continued to flourish; the plant capacity being regularly increased by the addition of boilers and generators. The GWR generated its own electricity for the railway works until 1925, when it agreed to take it entirely from the local authority's source. To allow for projected capacity, a new power station was approved in 1926. Opened at Moredon three years later, it was extended in 1942, and remained in use until 1973. Art Deco Corporation Electricity Showrooms were built in

Regent Circus, on the corner site which, at one time, was occupied by the Free Christian Church and the town's first museum collection.

On the transport front, private motor buses operated in Swindon and district from the 1920s, notably those of the Bristol Tramways (later Omnibus) Company that arrived in 1921. Its routes began at various points around Regent Circus, and over the years it built up a significant fleet. Here too, this company had offices and waiting rooms; initially they were on the east side of the square, and later to the south. As the main competitor to the Corporation's public transport, their buses were allowed to deposit passengers at the latter's fare stage stops, but could not pick up fares from them. The Corporation introduced some single-decker motor buses alongside its fleet of trams from 1927. These were the four-cylinder Lions, which Leyland developed in 1925. Two years later, the company launched its double-decker version of the Lions' six-cylinder sister, the Tiger, and called it the Titan. When, in 1929, a Swindon tram made the final trip, it was these that entirely replaced the Corporation's fleet. The Bristol Omnibus Company's activities continued to be centred on Regent Circus, and the Corporation's buses worked out of its depot until the Fleming Way bus station was opened in 1964.

Instructive and entertaining

There is hardly any information about the ways in which the people of the old town enjoyed themselves prior to the arrival of the railway. William Morris cites the annual fairs and feasts as the prime sources of jollification, and suggests that Swindonians had a liking for brutal sports. Occasionally there was dog-fighting, bull-baiting by dogs (popular until about 1812), wrestling or single stick playing, or a visit from strolling players. Many of these activities took place in the Market Square. Morris notes that bull-baiting was revived when the Wilts & Berks Canal was being built thereabouts, and said that single stick, or backsword, playing occurred until the early 1840s. Long after that, bare-knuckle fighting still took place in fields close by Swindon hostelries; George Strange (a relative by marriage of the present author) being one of the prime local exponents in the 1860s.

Of indoor public pastimes, the earliest mentioned appears to be a billiard room of 1842 in High Street; proprietor, Thomas Rose who was later to be in charge of the town's stamp office. By the 1860s, weekly United Free and Penny Readings (in fact they were free to 'the working classes') were taking place at the Old Swindon Town Hall, under the patronage of Ambrose Lethbridge Goddard. The pieces chosen were said to be 'instructive and entertaining' and there was also music and singing. At the same time, Isaac Ann (professor of music and pianoforte tuner) was holding choral classes.

Old Swindon was never as well served for entertainment as the new town. Such as there was, for example, the sisters Sophia and Annie's 1863

comic and musical entertainment at the Goddard Arms – entitled *Fun!* – took place either at hostelries on an ad hoc basis, in the Corn Exchange or the Town Hall. In 1892, the first provincial tour of the famous comedy *Charley's Aunt* came to the Corn Exchange, and the cast rehearsed at the Mason's Arms inn a few yards away. Apart from that, the prime mover in this area was the Mechanics Institution in New Swindon, discussed elsewhere. This very much set the precedent for enlightenment of the masses, according to the particular agenda of the institutional promoter. In the last few decades of the 19th century, the emphasis swung away from individually promoted events, and organised entertainment in Swindon became overtly educational. Much of it was taken over by the emerging churches, the new employers, and a whole range of 'improvement' committees. They were all providing centres for social gatherings and attempting to create a sense of community. Fundamental to this were the Friendly Societies; the Ancient Order of Foresters having established in 1843. By the turn of the century, their Court, Pride of Wiltshire, had long met at the King's Arms in Wood Street; Pride of Swindon was at the White Hart in Newport Street; and in New Swindon, Britain's Pride met at the Union Railway Hotel in Sheppard Street. The Mackies Good Intent Lodge of the Oddfellows was at the King's Arms, and The Widows' Hope Lodge moved between the Union Railway Hotel and the Locomotive Inn. The Freemasons were represented by the Royal Sussex Lodge of Emulation, No.355, at the Goddard Arms, and the Gooch Lodge No.1295 at the Queen's Royal Hotel. The Ancient Order of Shepherds' Loyal True Briton's Lodge met at the Foresters' Arms in Fleet Street; and at the Castle Inn, Prospect Place, could be found the United Patriots' National Benefit Society.

Non-conformists

The earliest Non-conformists in Swindon – that handful of religious dissenters recorded in 1676 – were probably Baptists who met as secretly as they could. Swindon seemed unwilling to approve of any alternative worship until at least the middle of the 19th century, after which time there was considerable pride in the widening religious mix, and much interest in the quality of the buildings they put up. Their initial reluctance was hardly surprising when Pleydell Goddard (Lord of the Manor 1732–42) seems to have been a prime mover in the disgraceful handling, by various Swindon mobs, of evangelist John Cennick and his supporters. The Wesleyan Methodist, John Pocock may have adopted a more subtle approach, and certainly seems not to have fallen foul of the manor. By the beginning of the 19th century, his followers, and a number of Independents, had obtained licensed meeting houses in the town. The Swindon Methodist Circuit was formed in 1817.

By the 1850s, there were three Non-conformist chapels associated with the old town and each had schoolrooms attached – the Baptists in Prospect Place, the Independents in Newport Street, and the Primitive Methodists at Eastcott. In New Swindon, Baptists, Primitive Methodists and Wesleyans were all well established. When the railway village was built, the Baptists moved into a house in Reading Street, from where they later removed to Westcott Place and then to the north end of Queen Street. They opened their first purpose-built chapel on the corner of Fleet Street and Bridge Street in 1849, although until the mid-1850s, this was administered from the then, 100-year-old establishment at Stratton Green, Stratton St Margaret. It was a single-storey, gabled building of ashlar with dressed quoins.

A number of religious sects met in 'iron churches' around the town, from time to time, but

Baptist Chapel, Fleet Street. The old town community of Baptists established themselves at Prospect Place. They came to Fleet Street, New Swindon in 1849, and it is a mark of the popularity of Baptism in Swindon, that within 30 years of being built, this substantial chapel could no longer accommodate its congregation. The Baptists gained as swift a stronghold in New Swindon as they had in the old town, and this, their first custom-built chapel hereabouts, reflected an optimism that proved to be not misplaced. They chose a prime site, centrally placed for both the developing railway village, the old community of Eastcott, and the residential building that was beginning to take place along the lane towards the Golden Lion Bridge and beyond. They came to Fleet Street in the care of Revd Richard Breeze of Bath Terrace, Old Swindon. The handsome Italianate chapel on the corner with Bridge Street, could seat 530. By the 1880s, the whole of Regent Street had been substantially built up, and the Baptists removed to their considerably grander, new tabernacle at the other end. Nothing remains of the Fleet Street chapel, except for part of the schoolroom (shown below) that adjoined it in Bridge Street.

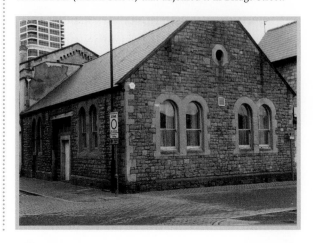

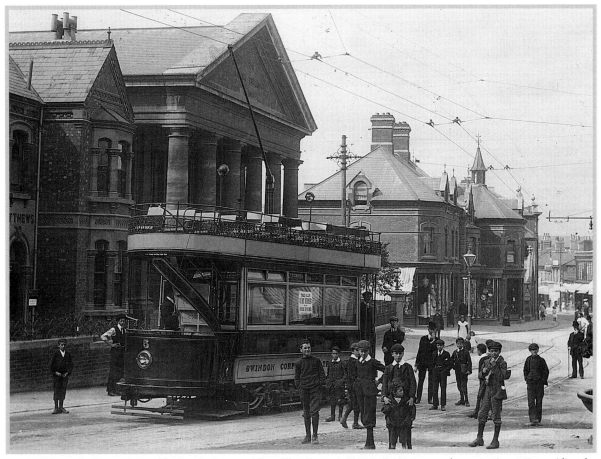

Baptist Tabernacle, Regent Street. The Baptists' removal from Fleet Street to Regent Street was another strategic move, providing the most notable building for public worship of the time in New Swindon. W.H. Read designed a distinguished classical building which was erected in 1886. It cost £6,000 and could accommodate 1,000 people. An impressive colonnade of six Tuscan columns supported a big pediment, enhanced by a flight of stone steps that ran the entire width of the front. Constructed of Bath stone, it occupied 3,589 sq.ft. with an additional 2,000 sq.ft. of schoolrooms. Those on the ground floor had partitions so that they could be opened out to provide for big occasions. The interior featured a gallery with ornamental front on three sides, supported on iron columns. Even after the Town Hall was built nearby five years later, the Baptist Tabernacle continued to dominate the southern end of Regent Street. The building was demolished in 1978, and in its place, the Pilgrim Centre began supplying succour and sustenance in 1990. The congregation here came from the Trinity Presbyterian Church that was built at the foot of Victoria Road in 1899, and is now a children's day nursery.

none was more interesting than the Free Christian Church that was opened in Bridge Street by Revd Frederick Rowland Young in 1861. It had a 32ft wide road frontage set back from a low wall, with poppy head railings, and a semi-circular roof, 15ft above ground level at its highest point. The sides were 10ft high. There was a little porch, lit by a single gas lamp, flanked by two, four-light windows. Inside were seats for up to 500 people, but no font, pulpit or communion table. A single bench sufficed; there was a harmonium and all the interior walls were covered with texts and illustrations from the scriptures. The church was established under the banner of Unitarianism, although Young disagreed with its teachings and withdrew from that body in 1875.

Within a year of opening, Young had built an adjacent school, employed J.G. Davis as master and acquired an assistant in Revd T. Noble. He also edited a monthly periodical, *The Christian Spiritualist*, and was frequently away on lecture tours. The congregation gradually declined and

Primitive Methodist Church, Regent Street. Primitive Methodism came to the area of New Swindon in the 1820s; a couple of decades before the new town was even thought of. When Upper Eastcott Farm stood with its outbuildings amidst narrow trackways, roughly where Regent Circus is today, Primitive Methodism took root in a nearby cottage. By means of a series of land conveyances, acquisitions from the Rolleston estate and private purchases, the Primitive Methodists were able to build their first New Swindon chapel at this isolated spot, enlarge it and add a schoolroom. In 1876, they opened a substantial building to seat 600, erected by George Wiltshire, to a design by Swindon architects Baker & Hinton. It was an imposing façade in red brick with Bath stone dressings and quoins, of seven bays with a central doorway, two flanking doors and flights of steps at right angles to Regent Street. Internally, the arrangement was similar to that of the Baptist Tabernacle; galleries all round, fronted by ornamental ironwork and supported on iron columns. There was a schoolroom beneath the chapel, and classrooms at the rear. Subsequently, road widening swept away the latter, necessitated some remodelling of the frontage and caused some new building to take place to the south-east of the original structure. What was a beautifully symmetrical building, now presented an ugly façade and appeared quite out of shape. A new Methodist Sunday school building was opened behind the chapel in 1895. These premises were seconded to the War Office during World War Two, and in 1946 were leased to Swindon Corporation and opened as an Arts Centre. It also accommodated the junior lending library and a meeting room. These remained there until the lease ran out ten years later.

Young put in plans to build a smaller church in Rolleston Street, and closed down the iron church in 1874. He sold the building almost at once, and it became a music hall and a skating rink before being sold to Arkell's Brewery. They re-erected it in St Philip's Road at Upper Stratton, where it was used as a beer store. Late in the 19th century, it became a chapel and then St Philip's Church. When the parish church of St Philip was built in Beechcroft Road in 1904, the iron church became the church hall. It was eventually demolished in the 1970s.

Meanwhile, Young held his services in follower Fred Davis' New Swindon auction yard for nearly a year, until his new Free Christian Church was opened in 1875 in Rolleston Street. It had been built in Decorated style with geometric traceried windows, of brick and stone with a slate roof, and a gabled frontage of random-coursed Swindon stone with Bath stone dressings. This building could accommodate just 200 on individual chairs, it measured 31ft wide by 50ft deep, and internally was quite unlike its predecessor. There was an altar and a pulpit; the former in front of a large traceried window with moulded arches springing from carved bosses. The ceiling was plastered and

Holy Rood Roman Catholic Church, Groundwell Road. Until 1851, when a chapel was opened in Bridge Street, New Swindon, Roman Catholic worshippers were poorly served hereabouts. They either had to travel to distant parishes or wait for a priest to say mass, once a month in the room at the Greyhound Inn, which was later to be used by the Welsh Congregationalists. In 1882, the Roman Catholics took over premises at the bottom of Rolleston Street, that had been designed in 1875 by Revd Frederick Rowland Young for his followers in the Free Christian Church. Four years later, Young built a splendid house adjacent to the chapel. Then he suddenly gave up his ministry, resigned his seat on the Old Swindon Local Board and left the town. This allowed the Roman Catholics to take over the church, which they refurbished and reopened in 1883. They remained on this corner site until 1905. Their flint built, Early English-style cruciform church of the Holy Rood, in Groundwell Road, cost £4,000 and was designed by E. Doran Webb. Originally it had chancel, nave, aisles and transepts but, in the 1970s, was realigned and extended.

painted blue, and the walls were stuccoed. At about this time, Young met Charles Anthony Wheeler, a chemist of High Street, Old Swindon, who built both the Hermitage, and Rose Cottage in Drove Road – and bought the latter from him in the parish reading room for an instant deposit of £30. He lived at Rose Cottage until 1879, when he was given local authority approval to build a substantial house adjoining his Free Christian Church. Almost at once, Young gave up his ministry, and the church building was bought by the Roman Catholics in 1882.

Mass employment in New Swindon

One of the earliest mass employers outside the railway industry in New Swindon was J. Compton's clothing factory in Sheppard Street. The company came to Swindon in 1871, occupying a cottage and employing ten people by the time it erected its factory on the same site. Designed by Swindon architect J.J. Smith, this fine piece of purpose-built industrial architecture was put up in 1876. It featured a 3,420 sq.ft. workroom, housing machinery for sewing, riveting and hot pressing. The company occupied women on a scale that previous employers had not, and was under contract to make railway and military uniforms out of supplied cloth. Within two years, 300 people were working at Compton's and the company was employing an army of home workers operating under piece rates. By the beginning of the 20th century, over 1,000 people worked there. The workforce expanded again during both wars, opening a sub-factory in Old Swindon during the second round of hostilities. The company became Compton, Son & Webb. A casualty of their success was the adjacent Union Tavern, one of the earliest hostelries to be built in

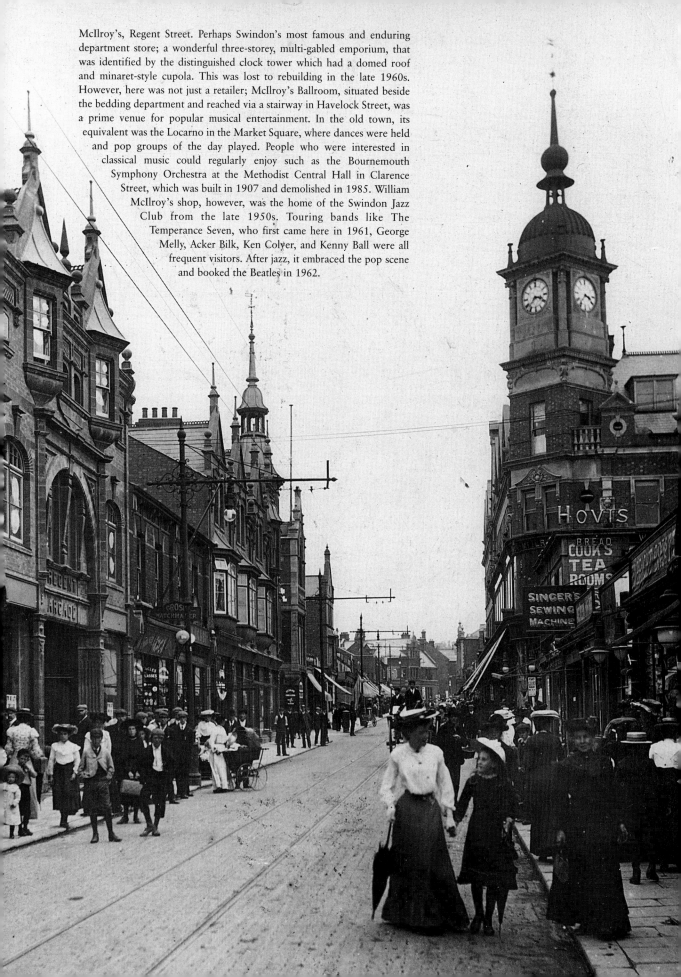

McIlroy's, Regent Street. Perhaps Swindon's most famous and enduring department store; a wonderful three-storey, multi-gabled emporium, that was identified by the distinguished clock tower which had a domed roof and minaret-style cupola. This was lost to rebuilding in the late 1960s. However, here was not just a retailer; McIlroy's Ballroom, situated beside the bedding department and reached via a stairway in Havelock Street, was a prime venue for popular musical entertainment. In the old town, its equivalent was the Locarno in the Market Square, where dances were held and pop groups of the day played. People who were interested in classical music could regularly enjoy such as the Bournemouth Symphony Orchestra at the Methodist Central Hall in Clarence Street, which was built in 1907 and demolished in 1985. William McIlroy's shop, however, was the home of the Swindon Jazz Club from the late 1950s. Touring bands like The Temperance Seven, who first came here in 1961, George Melly, Acker Bilk, Ken Colyer, and Kenny Ball were all frequent visitors. After jazz, it embraced the pop scene and booked the Beatles in 1962.

MASS EMPLOYMENT IN NEW SWINDON

The College, Victoria Road. Until the 20th century, technical education had been largely in the hands of the Council of the Mechanics Institution, who ran suitable courses at a number of venues. During the 1890s, they discussed the possibility of establishing a permanent technical institution with the Wiltshire Education Committee, to be run under the auspices of a local technical education committee. About a dozen major schools were operating in Swindon in 1895 when the Swindon and North Wiltshire Technical Institution was opened, designed by Silcock & Reay. It was primarily established to provide engineering classes for the GWR's students. An imposing, sombre building of red bricks with Dutch gables, in the favoured manner at the time, most of its decorative interest was concentrated on the built-out central section. It cost about £14,000 which was paid for by a combination of the rates, a grant from the Wiltshire County Council and another from the Department of Science and Art in London. Swindon had a School Board from 1877, and formed an Education Committee when the former was abolished in 1902. The Mechanics Institution's involvement in technical education passed to the Education Committee of the town's Council, under the Education Act, 1902. Twenty-four years later, the Technical Institution was refurbished internally, and reorganised as a College of Further Education. It was named The College in 1927. By the late 1950s, Swindon had lost a number of terraces – namely Edmund Street, Horsell Street, and most of Byron Street and Rolleston Street – to make way for a car park and a six-storey college extension. This was a new multi-storey building, designed by Charles Pike & Partners and built between Victoria Road and Regent Circus. It was opened by the Duke of Edinburgh in 1961.

New Swindon. It was bought up, closed in 1958 and demolished so that Compton's could expand.

In 1901, the Cellular Clothing Company came to Swindon, using female labour to make pyjamas, sportswear and underwear. Eighteen years later, raincoat manufacturers Nicholsons Ltd set up in a former sweet factory in Manchester Road, that had also been used by Compton's. Nicholsons

made raincoats from supplied, pre-cut material. Another large employer of women was W.D. & H.O. Wills' tobacco and cigarette factory that opened in Colbourne Street in 1915 but was, towards the end of World War One, given over for a while to making ammunition cases. The Swindon factory closed in 1987.

From the second decade of the 20th century, light industry began to establish in and around the town. In 1919, the Garrard Engineering and Manufacturing Company came to Newcastle Street, where it manufactured gramophones. It closed down 60 years later and the building was demolished in 1984. During the war, Garrard's manufactured a variety of military equipment. One of the worst fires in Swindon occurred there in 1958, but although it had a devastating effect on the assembly and despatch areas in particular, the company swiftly recovered. The Plessey

The Southern Laundry. In the 1870s, the Aylesbury Dairy Company opened a milk processing and cheese-making factory on the corner of Station Road and Aylesbury Street, in a double-block, custom-designed factory of red brick with Bath stone dressings by W.H. Read, the Swindon architect. The company had been established seven years earlier by Buckinghamshire farmer G. Mander Allender, owner of prize Berkshire pigs, and the maker of renowned butter from his herd of Alderneys. It took milk from dairy farms in the district, and processed upwards of 2,000 gallons of milk each day at Swindon, in 400 sq.ft. pans. Some 500 quarts of cream were produced daily, and sent to markets in London. The skimmed milk was treated and made into about three tons of cheese per week. The company fed nearly 600 pigs in its nearby piggeries, with whey and other waste products from the various processes. These premises were later taken over by the Southern Laundry.

Sheppard Street. John Harding Sheppard, who sold the field immediately east of the railway village to speculative developers in the 1870s, required that the new streets should be named after him. At the east end of the street was the third bridge going north on the North Wilts Canal; Union Bridge or Bullen's Bridge. Close by were Compton's Clothing Factory and the railwaymen's Union Tavern which Sheppard had built on his own land in 1840.

Company, makers of radio components, relocated to a factory in Kembrey Street in 1940. In 1942, the Admiralty moved a ships' gun mountings factory into Petter Engines' premises just north of Swindon. This was Marine Mountings, later occupied by R.A. Lister & Co. for making various types of motors. At about the same time, Vickers-Armstrong came to South Marston on the south-eastern outskirts of the town, where they made Supermarine Spitfires during World War Two. Later, they manufactured several jet fighters before the works diversified into several industrial divisions. The site became an industrial park from the 1970s, used mainly for light engineering, warehousing and distribution.

Cricket and football

The earliest organised sport was cricket in the old town which, certainly by the 1850s, was well established. There was a cricket ground that had formerly been part of Okus Farm and, throughout the later 19th century, was leased by the Goddards to various individuals. In 1885, A.L. Goddard also leased a piece of land in Cricklade Road to, amongst others, Revd Maurice Ponsonby of St Mark's, for use as a cricket field. Over the years, cricket, football, polo, and bicycling became popular outdoor pursuits. In 1881, the Old Swindon Cricket Club played a game of football with the lads of St Mark's Young Men's Friendly Society. Immediately afterwards, the two sides joined forces, apparently at the suggestion of Revd William Pitt, and became the Swindon Town Football Club. As an amateur outfit, they played on various unsuitable fields around the old town, before establishing themselves at the Croft in 1884. In those days, they played in green shirts and changed at the Fountain public house in Devizes Road. At Croft, they began to engage professional players and were founder members of the Southern League Division One. Four years

later, it was said of them: 'Now established on a professional basis (STFC) has failed lamentably to justify the expectations of those who had faith in professionalism, and its record for the season, it must be confessed, is a poor one compared with that of former years when the club existed on an amateur basis'. The club moved to the County Ground in 1896, and has since remained there. In 1920, it became a founder member of Division Three (South), where the team played until 1963

The Cricket Pavilion, County Ground, County Road. A group of gentry and businessmen established the Swindon Cricket Club in 1844, although there is mention that the game was played in Swindon over two decades earlier. The earliest surviving record is the Treasurer's Book of 1854; it shows that a decade after the club was formed, it was still the preserve of the town's more profitable traders. The club played on various grounds, notably in a field close by Drove Road, and later at The Sands. There in 1872, some five years after they changed their name to Old Swindon Cricket Club, a pavilion was built which initially had a thatched roof. Two years later, they were renamed the Swindon Rangers Cricket Club. In 1893, hardly any roads had been built up east of Corporation Street. The only exceptions were the railway workers' terrace in Gooch Street, immediately to the south of the railway line, and Cetus Buildings on the north side of the Wilts & Berks Canal. In that year, Swindon's outdoor, multi-sports complex was opened, about one third of a mile due east of the expanding town. The 29-acre County Ground, off the old drovers' road, comprised football pitch, cricket ground with pavilion, and peripheral bicycle track, one-third of a mile round. It was also used as a racecourse and polo ground. The 1893 cricket pavilion survives; an elaborate two-storey, nine-bay structure of wood and brick, held up by a cast-iron arcade and having gabled rooms at each end. It cost £850 to build. It was designed by W.H. Read and E.H. Pritchett. The competitors' changing rooms opposite the pavilion, added £450, and the lodge house that guarded the complex, a further £250. A 12½ acre extension to the County Ground was opened in 1930.

when they gained promotion for the first time. The club won the Football League Cup Final at Wembley in 1969, and the Anglo-Italian Cup the following year. In 1993–4 they enjoyed one season in the FA Premiership.

The most famous person associated with the club was Harold Fleming who was capped nine times for England between 1907 and 1924. In later years, he had a sports shop in Regent Circus; the precedent for the Faringdon Road emporium of Don Rogers, the club's more recent celebrity footballer.

Entertainment

Entertainment in the railway village initially centred on the GWR works, where theatrical performances, musical events and dances took place, in part of the paint shop at the locomotive works. Soon after the Mechanics Institution was built, it was offering seasons that included musical entertainments and dramatic performances. By 1900, lantern slide shows – still images projected on to a screen – were regular attractions at the Mechanics Institution, in an arcade in Regent Street and at the Corn Exchange in the old town. These were soon followed by black and white, moving newsreels, shown at the same venues.

It is believed that c.1908, an open-air café in Regent Circus set up a screen and began showing films on a fairly regular basis. This led to Swindon's first indoor cinema, the Picture House, created c.1910 in a former insurance office that stood on the east side of Regent Circus. The building had been modified; it seated 400 and claimed to be the only one of its type in Europe with a sliding roof, for the convenience of patrons on hot days. The Picture House closed down in 1913, was converted for use as a roller skating rink and by 1918 had become a garage. In the 1920s, this building doubled as the waiting office

for the Bristol Tramways and Carriage Company, and J. Mitchell's florist shop. Meanwhile, Swindon's first custom-built cinema, the County Electric Pavilion, was built in Regent Street in 1910, on part of the site occupied by present-day Woolworths. This was followed in 1911 by the Central Cinema in Fleet Street and, a few months later, by the 1,000-seat Arcadia, which was built on the site of the Regent arcade of shops. The Arcadia featured its own orchestra. It became the Classic Cinema in the 1950s, then the Classic Cartoon Cinema, and was demolished in 1974 after a period as a bingo hall. The County Electric closed c.1926, the Central in 1930.

In 1914, the Electra Palace cinema opened in the Swindon suburb of Gorse Hill, where a reduction in the seat price could be had by those who produced their tram ticket as proof they had travelled some distance to attend. The Regent Cinema opened in 1929, next to the site of the Picture House. It could accommodate 1,322 people and during its history as a cinema, was also titled the Gaumont, and from 1962 the Odeon. When it opened, it claimed to be the first talking cinematography theatre in the county, and featured a Compton Wonder Organ. When it closed as a cinema in 1974, the Odeon became a bingo hall. The Art Deco-style Savoy cinema, was built less than 200 yards distant, next to the Rifleman's Arms public house, in 1937. It was designed by W.R. Glen, had a seating capacity of 1,775 and was notable for its Saturday morning children's film club. It became the ABC, was the Cannon for its last five years, and closed in 1991. In 1930, the little 620-seat Palladium Picture House was built in Jennings Street, in the suburb of Rodbourne. It was to remain in business for less than 30 years. There are now no cinemas in central Swindon, the role having been taken over by multi-screen complexes on the western and eastern outskirts of the town.

A number of popular, small bands established in Swindon during the 1920s and 1930s, but it was during the 1940s and 1950s that the town really embraced the dance hall culture. The swimming baths became the Majestic Ballroom, where national touring bands, like that of Victor Silvester, came to play. The Regal was actually the auditorium of the Playhouse Theatre in part of the Mechanics Institution, the Locarno Dance Hall packed them into the old Corn Exchange, and McIlroy's Ballroom was 'where it was at', in Regent Street. Dances continued to be held, as they had during the war years, in many smaller venues such as the Bradford Hall in Devizes Road, and other church halls. The former was unusual in having its chairs and tables, rather than the band, on the balcony, with dancing on the floor below. These were the years of Swindon bands led by Harry Smith, Johnny Stiles (who later became landlord of the White Hart at Stratton St Margaret), Ken Kitching and Gordon Talbot.

The town's theatres

The Swindon Museum has a record of a playbill of 1829 that refers to a theatre in Swindon, and mentions boxes and a gallery. Yet the site of this is unknown, and no other evidence of its existence has come to light.

The Queen's, to be called the Empire Theatre from 1906, was built in red brick on a 10,350 sq.ft. site at the foot of Victoria Road in 1897/98, to the design of Bristol architects, Drake & Pizey. It cost £10,000 and was originally under the management of Ernest Carpenter, a theatre professional from Bristol. Its great pediments, finials and cupolas made it one of the town's major buildings. The auditorium, which had nine exits, seated 1,600 people arranged in the stalls, dress circle, upper circle, and above this a number of seats known locally as 'the gods'. The stage was

The Empire Theatre. Designed by the man who conceived the New Swindon Town Hall, and built in 1897, the Queen's Theatre (later the Empire) had a far more restrained façade than its contemporary and, sadly, a less imposing position. Even so, Brightwen Binyon gave it corner turrets, a range of pinnacles, drop pediments and a massive, central pediment. It was built of red brick with stone details and eventually had an attractive canopy over its corner doors. The theatre was replaced in 1960 by Empire House, a characterless block of offices and shops on the same site.

55ft wide by 35ft deep, with a proscenium of 29ft at the centre. The theatre was notable for its interior decoration, mouldings, and a succession of interesting safety curtains packed with advertisements. When the Regent cinema opened in 1929, theatre audiences dropped to such a degree that, for the next 18 years, the Empire also turned to talking pictures, with its only stage show being the annual Christmas pantomime. In 1947, live variety and musical entertainments came back to the stage. Yet whilst it did have well-known rising stars of the day, it rarely attracted the best acts, and was noted for the frequency with which certain performers reappeared. It was apocryphally, but widely, said to receive only the 'B' circuit shows. Its resident pit orchestra in the late 1940s and 1950s was composed of part-time musicians, of which the long-time musical director, Tim Coxon, was by day, a mechanic at the nearby Victoria Garage. It was also maintained that the dressing room accommodation and backstage facilities left much to be desired. The

The Wyvern Theatre, Theatre Square. This was the first building to be completed in Swindon's £7.5 million Civic Centre Project that began in the late 1960s. It opened in 1971, following a topping out ceremony the previous year by the Mayor of Swindon, Alderman John Pass. There was a Swindon Corporation-sponsored competition to select a name for the theatre; 200 entries were received and Jo Hodgkinson – one-time director of the Swindon Playhouse in the Mechanics Institution and then recently retired drama director of the Arts Council of Great Britain – chose the winning name. It was found that two people had submitted 'Wyvern'; these were former Wiltshire County Councillor Kenneth Bolton, and Swindon resident Sydney Cook. In a ballot conducted by the Mayor, Mr Bolton won. The wyvern design on the Theatre Square elevation is from the drawing by Edward Bawden, formerly an official war artist who made drawings of the evacuation from Dunkirk. The proscenium opening is 35ft, and the depth of the stage 30ft, extending to 41ft. The width of the stage and wings is 77ft, and the fly tower is 57ft high. The first administrator of the theatre was Brien Chitty who came from the Newcastle Playhouse. The theatre opened in September 1971 with a musical spectacular by the Ukranian Dance Company, before an invited audience of over 600 people. This was the Company's first visit to Britain, and they packed the theatre for a two-week run. The first box office manager was Wilton Morley, son of actor Robert Morley, and publicity was in the hands of Mary Morgan who came from the Belgrade Theatre, Coventry.

Empire closed during a run of the pantomime Robinson Crusoe in 1955, and was demolished four years later. The name is remembered in Empire House, the shop and office block that replaced it on the same site in 1960.

Swindon's 'other' professional theatre is at the Arts Centre in Devizes Road. The Borough of Swindon's policy of supporting the arts led, in 1946, to the opening of a dedicated arts centre in a converted Sunday school building in Regent Street. It accommodated the ancillary societies;

the groups of like-minded individuals, that had established after the war to celebrate and learn about specific areas of the arts. It also enabled exhibitions, concerts and theatre productions to be staged in a small way. For several decades, almost all arts centre activities were of an amateur nature. Meanwhile, in 1956, the Arts Centre removed to the adapted Bradford Hall, the Council-owned property it occupies today. There is a 240-seat theatre where professional artists, and stage shows that suit such an intimate environment, can be seen.

Arts Centre, Devizes Road. In 1946, Harold Jolliffe, Swindon's then recently-appointed Borough Librarian, opened the first municipal arts centre in the UK, following a scheme that had been approved and was being developed during the time of his predecessor. The centre, in a converted former Methodist schoolroom, was hired out to such educational and cultural bodies as were deemed suitable by the aldermen and councillors who made up the Public Libraries, Museums and Arts Committee. Everything that went on there fell under the heading of 'public library extension activities' and the hiring organisations were collectively known as 'ancillary societies'. When the lease expired in 1956, the council-owned Bradford Hall in Devizes took over. This venue had a 240-seat theatre and was famed for its excruciatingly slow curtain. It also had committee rooms, meeting rooms, offices and a club room – indicative of the kinds of activities that had built up over the years. The town's societies used the centre as a meeting place, and the theatre was used for recitals, talks and programmes of an improving nature. A request in the 1960s to hire it for a striptease show (even though the famous Phyllis Dixey had previously played the Empire) was met with outrage amongst the good burghers of the town! As late as the early 1990s, there was no professional programming. In 1993, Clarry Bean took over the complex and immediately set about turning it into a vibrant and exciting venue, attracting first-class acts, touring companies and contemporary theatre.

Swindon was without a replacement for the Empire until the 658-seat Wyvern was opened in 1971, built in Theatre Square adjacent to Regent Circus, to an award-winning design by Casson, Conder & Partners. Its dragon logostyle was designed by Edward Bawden, a former official war artist of Saffron Walden, Essex. As well as the auditorium proper, the complex featured a members' club room and the Jolliffe Studio – a space for experimental theatre named in memory of Harold Jolliffe (1914–1969). He was Swindon's borough librarian from 1946 until his death, an author, one of the luminaries of the UK public library profession, and specialised in public 'extension activities'. These included the borough-owned Wyvern Theatre which was originally intended to fall under his auspices. It specialised in week-long runs, and was successful in bringing to Swindon some of the best drama and musical productions the town has ever seen. Sadly, the theatre is not large enough to accommodate audiences of sufficient size to attract the kind of performers the town's younger patrons would like to see. Ironically, the audiences for the excellent theatrical productions of its first decade dwindled, and the theatre was eventually sold to the Apollo group of theatres.

Post-war expansion

Just before World War Two, Swindon had a working population of 36,000, of whom 4,000 were in retailing and around 15,000 were employed in the railway's works and offices. Its town clerk, appointed 1937, was David Murray John, who is remembered today in the Canal Walk tower block that bears his name. He was a small man with a huge vision, (though this didn't extend to every health issue as he was rarely seen without a cigarette). He became the virtual architect of the town's post-war growth, and the founder of

modern Swindon. His mission was to facilitate significant alternative employment to the railway works. It meant encouraging a diversity of inward investment that would create jobs, and providing housing for the new workers. Ironically, central government rejected the first application by Swindon's immediate post-war Council to create a new town.

When the Town Development Act was passed in 1952, the Council was able to make out a persuasive case for Swindon as an 'overspill' district, ideally suited to accommodate a good number of London's jobless who were also experiencing difficult living conditions. The Act provided for rehousing subsidies, the compulsory purchase of land, and financial assistance from government towards amenities and services. Negotiations were successful between Swindon's Council, the London County Council and the Borough of Tottenham. Murray John and his officers set about a programme of diversification that would expand the town's industrial base, regenerate its post-war economy, and significantly increase the Council's housing stock. Plessey and Vickers helped to inaugurate the programme by agreeing to employ 1,500 of the new intake of workers. In a two-pronged attack, separate peripheral sites were found for industrial parks and housing developments. The net result of this policy was that in the three decades from 1951, Swindon's population grew by a staggering 70 per cent; some 58 per cent higher than the national average over the same period. David Murray John died in 1974.

Swindon did not see a lot of residential development in the early decades of the 20th century. Pinehurst, on the town's north-eastern edge with Stratton St Margaret, had been built up in the late 1920s/early 1930s, and at the end of that decade, a handful of roads that became known as Old Walcot were put in, east of Drove

Road leading from the old town. The first residential area to be developed after World War Two was at Rodbourne Cheney, built in 1947 on land adjacent to the allotments. Swindon's housing estates proper began with Penhill, put up to the north of the town between 1952 and 1955, with the London overspill very much in mind. This was followed by a remarkable amount of residential building in a very short space of time, mostly to the east of the old Drove (drovers') Road out of High Swindon, and north of the road to Marlborough. The Lawns, erected on what was once part of the Goddard estate and named after the family's home, was a gradual development that began in 1954. The Walcot estate, was begun to the east of Old Walcot in 1956 and was completed by the end of the decade. Park South was built to the north-east of the Lawns 1956–64, and Park North was developed mainly between 1957 and 1961.

It was in the 1950s that Swindon lost its insularity. At the start of the decade, the population figure for the Borough was around 90,000. The local authority welcomed immigrants and accommodated them more readily than many Swindonians, who held the opinion that natives of the town should be preferred in all matters. This included local authority housing, of which there was insufficient, and schools that were too few and in

The Cenotaph, Regent Circus. The town's first memorial to the hostilities of World War One was a wooden 'peace' flagpole. This was burned down in 1922 by rioters who started the fire using a can of petrol, 'obtained' from an innocent motorist driving around the Town Hall. A policeman caught the flag as it came down, and the rioters paraded the pole through the shopping centre. It was replaced, near to the junction with Princes Street, by a short, wooden obelisk, painted white. This had been in the course of construction as early as 1916; a private venture on the part of a Corporation carpenter who had lost his son during fighting the year before. In its turn, the obelisk was replaced later in 1922 by a cenotaph on the Regent Street side, made of Portland stone.

the wrong areas. Utilitarian business premises appeared on brownfield sites; buildings that accommodated need in the most cost-effective way, with little regard for the aesthetic effect on the townscape. Within a decade or so, many of the buildings that had been developed or remodelled over a century or more, gave way to ghastly 1960s kitsch. Interesting Regent Street shop frontages, hardly changed since they were packed with the wares of their proud Victorian or Edwardian family owners for the photograph album, were replaced by sterile anonymity. First-floor Victorian house façades remained in many cases, but they were overwhelmed by the architectural vandalism at street level.

In many instances, individuality gave way to corporate design as the small retail chains moved in. Central Swindon closed down after six o'clock in the evening. It used to be said that only the pubs, the cinemas and the libraries were open later. Even after night clubs were introduced, Swindon did not really have a night life comparable with other aspiring cities until the theme bar culture took off in the 1990s.

If the 1950s were to be unsettling for the population, it was nothing to the changes of the next decade. The Council embarked on a huge programme of clearance and rebuilding. Part of this resulted in the Courts of Justice and the adjacent car parks being built in an area where there had been a number of brothels until the mid-1960s. Meanwhile, the old town was being systematically taken apart; historic buildings were destroyed in advance of road-widening schemes and car park construction, or simply because new build was a more cost-effective alternative to restoration. It was a rationale based on the perceived needs of the day – to increase the population, facilitate traffic flow, and build a utilitarian environment and infrastructure that would at least do for the moment. The old town never recovered from this, nor has it ever achieved the kind of secure economic autonomy that could have come in later years by refurbishing and remodelling those buildings. It could have

been the key to the kind of tourism that Swindon now craves.

The jewel in the town's crown was to be the Parade shopping development that physically changed the shape of town centre retailing. It was heralded by redevelopment along the line of the canal in the vicinity of Regent Street, that swept away a number of late 19th-century terraces. The Parade was laid out at the beginning of the 1970s, and was extended in 1975. Such was the rush for renewal, that roads such as Wellington Street, which abutted the Fleming Way development, were also demolished at this time. Very little of the new town escaped redevelopment during this period, which also saw the first of the multi-storey buildings (such as the Hambro Life offices of the late 1960s) going up. Central Swindon became a building site, and developers reached for the sky. Swindon's tallest building to date, the David Murray John tower which dominates the central area, was built in 1976 as part of the planned construction of The Parade.

The later 1960s and early 1970s saw a continuation of residential developments eastwards. Nythe, Eldene and Liden took outer Swindon as far as it could go in this direction. Between 1976 and the late 1990s, most of Swindon's residential development was in an area north of the Wootton Bassett Road, bounded by Rodbourne in the east and the Lydiards to the west. This vast area includes several residential districts that began in the late 1970s with Toothill, which the Council built, for sale or rent, to the south. House building by private developers then moved northwards, curling around central Swindon in a crescent shape. Freshbrook, West Swindon and Westlea were all put up in the early 1980s, Grange Park by mid-decade, The Prinnels and Sparcells near the end of it. Then the western development pushed north, right up against its boundary with North Wiltshire, abutting Lydiard

Country Park and adjacent to the boundary with Lydiard Tregoze. Eastleaze, Ramleaze, Middleleaze and Nine Elms had culminated at Peatmoor by the late 1990s.

Most of these areas follow the same sort of pattern that was adopted half a century before – self-contained communities with their own shops, surgeries, places of worship, and social centres. From the late 1990s, there have been residential developments, particularly in the old town, aimed at bringing homeowners back to the High Street area. But elsewhere, Swindon is now in effect a number of large suburban villages. At the end of the 1990s came the great push of the private sector-led northern residential expansion towards Blunsdon, ultimately to provide an additional 10,000 homes. In 2001, plans were put forward to build on Swindon's 'front garden', its strip of green belt adjacent to the M4 motorway.

The gradual expansion of Swindon throughout the second half of the 20th century, was for a long time, simply to provide homes for employees of the companies that were attracted to the town. By 1968, a plan had been drawn up that would have turned Swindon into a new city west of London, accommodated an additional 75,000 people from London within 13 years, and given it a population of some 310,000 by the end of the 20th century. This was scaled down, but it formed the basis of the western and northern expansions of the existing town. The M4 motorway arrived in 1971, and thereafter Swindon itself became a satellite town, within easy reach of others along the motorway corridor and, in many instances, a less expensive place in which to live. During the 1990s, there was a housing recession and consequently a slowdown in the rate of growth. The predicted northern residential expansion was also slow to start. At the end of the 20th century, Swindon was a town in which thousands of workers employed between London and South

Wales have homes. In 2002, the population figure for the Borough stood at 181,000.

A radical change

The story of Swindon during the last two decades of the 20th century depended more than anything else on diversifying its business base and attracting inward investment. Until the 1940s, most of the businesses in the town could still be traced back to their family origins, in many instances established during the 19th century. From World War Two until the 1970s, it was mostly well-known UK engineering companies that set up in the town. Mass employer Pressed Steel Fisher established its car body pressing and assembly plant in 1955, giving a huge boost to Swindon's engineering workforce. This subsequently became a Rover car body and pressings plant. The town's motor vehicle association was increased 30 years later when Honda opened a pre-delivery inspection facility for their Rover-assembled cars. In 1989, it opened an engine manufacturing plant on the site of the former Vickers aircraft factory, and in 1992 the massive car-making plant came on stream as Honda of the UK Manufacturing. Rover was acquired by the German carmaker BMW in 1994. In 2000, Honda added a second, adjacent manufacturing plant. Although Swindon is no longer dependent on a single employer, or indeed any one employment sector, the town's motor car industry draws many parallels with the heyday of the GWR.

Newsagent and bookseller W.H. Smith & Son brought their national supply centre to Swindon in 1963, and in 1967 their direct mail arm – Book Club Associates – opened, later adding its own warehouse. In 1973, Burmah Castrol joined the swelling ranks of international organisations bringing their headquarters to Swindon. Once the town's communication links were established and

Queen's Park. In 1950, a garden of remembrance to Swindon's war dead was opened just off Drove Road. The area around it, formerly Thomas Turner's clay pits, was converted into ornamental gardens. A lake was created, walkways were put in and the whole area was planted up and opened as Queen's Park in 1953. Work continued throughout the 1960s, and at its best, Queen's Park also included rose gardens and a fine hothouse full of tropical plants. Neither remain intact; the latter having been partly demolished during the late 1980s and early 90s. Part of the perimeter walkway was closed in the earlier decade due to slippage, and financial constraints have since precluded repairs. Even so, this is the most frequently used of the town's parks, and is a favourite of office workers at lunchtimes. It has fine lawns, some excellent specimen trees and shrubs, big herbaceous borders and the wildfowl lake and island. The park is dedicated to Maurice J. Williams (1910-88), who was formerly the town's Parks Superintendent responsible for its design (with then Borough Architect J. Loring-Morgan) and layout. He is commemorated on a plaque at the Groundwell Road entrance.

understood, the town became a site for warehousing and distribution companies; national and global distributors like Renault, PHH (now Arval PHH) and MAN Bus & Truck.

In the 1950s, work began on the town's first business park, for commercial and light units. It was sited at Okus, in the middle of the area formerly known as The Sands. This was followed by Cheney Manor to the north-east of the town centre in 1955. From 1971, the M4, with its links to other motorways and arterial routes, meant that Swindon could present itself as being at the hub of road and rail networks and ideally placed to

service the whole M4 corridor. From the mid-1960s, it has seriously pursued a policy of building industrial estates, and office and business parks, to continue attracting incoming industry. In the year 2000, there were 40 of them, the largest being the old Vickers Armstrong site at South Marston, adjacent to the two massive Honda of the UK Manufacturing plants.

The policy of diversification really took off in the 1980s, as Swindon became the fastest growing town in Europe. It was attracting industries at the cutting edge of emerging technologies, global players and foreign investment. Currently, the town deals in information technology and communication, manufacturing, financial services, distribution and direct mail. In 2001, there were over 50 American companies in the town, more than 40 European businesses from eight different countries, and a significant number from the Far East.

Even though the 19th-century railway navvies must have seemed a race apart to the occupants of the old town, nothing in the town's previous history so dramatically changed its socio-economic pattern, or its population mix, as its astonishing business growth in the 1990s. Many of the most desirable organisations were concerned with

telecommunications, information technology, technological innovation and multimedia. It would all be incomprehensible to the architects of the town's immediate post-war development.

The city campaign

The first initiative to acquire city status for Swindon began in the early 1990s as a co-operative venture between the then Borough of Thamesdown and the Swindon Chamber of Commerce. Twice before had County Borough status been advanced, in the period before

Lydiard Park House is Swindon's only stately home. It was purchased by Swindon Corporation in 1943; restored and refurbished and opened to the public in 1955. When the mediaeval village of Lydiard Tregoze disappeared in the 1600s, it left a church and a mediaeval-style, cross-winged hall house that was remodelled during the 1740s using the dowry that Anne Furnese brought to her marriage with the 2nd Viscount St John. The 1st Viscount, created 1712, was the Tory statesman Henry St John, Secretary of State to Queen Anne. Diana Spencer, daughter of the Duke of Marlborough, caused a national scandal when she divorced Frederick, 2nd Viscount Bolingbroke in 1768, and considerably more disquiet when she went on to marry the great-grandson of Charles II's liaison with Nell Gwynne. During the last century of their incumbency, the family sold much of the furniture from the state rooms, and there has been an ongoing and very successful programme to find and restore original St John furnishings, china, silver, glassware and personal artefacts. Associated with the 1939-45 war, there were variously an American servicemen's camp, a military hospital, a prisoner of war hospital and a housing estate in the grounds. In 1962, the 6th Viscount Bolingbroke loaned back his picture collection and this was eventually bought by Swindon Corporation for permanent display. The house has state rooms with fine Rococo ceilings, portrait-hung walls and classical settings.

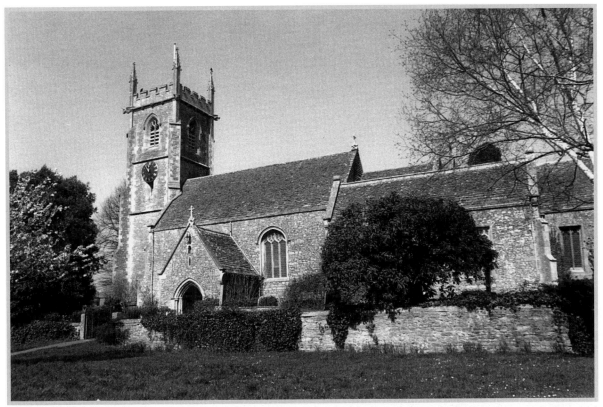

St Mary, Rodbourne Cheney. This church has an interesting piece of local folklore, in that a golden altar was supposedly buried hereabouts and then forgotten. It has some Anglo-Saxon decoration, but is 13th-century at its core and 15th-century elsewhere. The church was restored in 1848 at a cost of £3,000 by the Swindon architect Sampson Sage who lived in Prospect Place, and everywhere the 19th and 20th centuries are inescapable. Happily, it looks like a proper church; chancel, nave, north aisle, south porch and embattled western tower, although it had a central tower before the restoration. There are monuments from the 17th, 18th and 19th centuries inside the church, and also in the churchyard which has some nice chest tombs.

amalgamation in 1900, and again during Swindon's unprecedented expansion at the end of the 1950s. By the 1990s, Swindon was one of the most important centres along the M4 corridor. Throughout the last decade of the 20th century, the town continued to be a magnet for new, high-tech businesses and relocating companies, and the focus of major business expansion. However, its infrastructure and amenities did not develop at a correspondingly satisfactory level. The Borough Council published *2030 Starts Here*, an overview of the town's urban regeneration needs; and by 2002, Swindon's bid for city status had twice been rejected. An Urban Regeneration Company was set up to create a blueprint for revitalising much of the central area by means of desirable redevelopment of brownfield sites. At the same time, the private joint owners of the Brunel shopping centre published extensive plans to rebuild the retail face of Swindon.

Never before in the town's history of piecemeal development has there been such a need for change, on so great a scale; or for every issue to be dealt with as part of an integrated whole. The prospects for Swindon are exciting, and the opportunities endless.

AFTERWORD

This book will have achieved little if it does not make the reader eager for more. And through the work of gifted enthusiasts there is much more to be had, although it may not have been published in the usual way. The best work has been done by people with an interest in a specific topic or area of local history research, who have ransacked archives for documents and other primary source material, and trawled endlessly through newspapers and directories, extracting every piece of relevant information. Their manuscripts, are the body and soul of local history research.

I am referring to volumes like Trevor Cockbill's *Finest Things Out*, a passionate and wonderfully rambling year-by-year account of the Mechanics Institution. If you want to know what life was like for real people, Joe Silto achieves this admirably in *A Swindon History 1840–1901* and *The Railway Town*. In *Home Brewed*, David Backhouse gives a comprehensive history of the area's breweries and public houses. Swindon Reference Library is the place to start. Simply ask what the library has on your preferred topic of local interest, and you may be amazed by what you get. But if no one has investigated and written up your particular sphere of interest, or you feel you can improve on what you find there, why not undertake your own research. The thrill of the chase is compelling. It may lead you down avenues of research you never dreamed of, and into contact with interesting people you would not otherwise meet. And the elation is beyond words when you discover something – as you will – that disproves a long-held belief, or simply adds another fact to what is already known.

INDEX